VISUAL QUICKSTART GUIDE

iMOVIE 2

FOR MACINTOSH

Jeff Carlson

Peachpit Press

Visual QuickStart Guide
iMovie 2 for Macintosh
Jeff Carlson

Peachpit Press

1249 Eighth Street
Berkeley, CA 94710
510/524-2178
800/283-9444
510/524-2221 (fax)
Find us on the World Wide Web at: http://www.peachpit.com
To report errors, send a note to errata@peachpit.com
Peachpit Press is a division of Pearson Education

Copyright © 2002 by Jeff Carlson

Editor: Nancy Davis
Production Coordinator: Connie Jeung-Mills
Copyeditor: Brooke Wheeler
Illustrations: Jeff Carlson, Jeff Tolbert
Compositor: Jeff Carlson
Indexer: Caroline Parks
Cover Design: The Visual Group

Notice of liability

The information in this book is distributed on an "As Is" basis, without warranty.
While every precaution has been taken in the preparation of the book, neither the
author nor Peachpit Press shall have any liability to any person or entity with respect
to any loss or damage caused or alleged to be caused directly or indirectly by the
instructions contained in this book or by the computer software and hardware
products described in it.

Trademarks

Visual QuickStart Guide is a registered trademark of Peachpit Press, a division of
Pearson Education. Peachpit Press is not affiliated with Apple Computer, Inc., Canon
U.S.A., Inc., Sony, Inc., or other companies whose products are featured in this book.
iMovie is copyright 1999-2001 Apple Computer. iMovie, iTunes, iDVD, and DVD Studio
Pro are registered trademarks of Apple Computer, Inc.

ISBN 0-201-78788-1

9 8 7 6 5 4 3 2 1

Printed and bound in the United States of America

Dedication

To Leonard, whose one-month film class at Whitworth instilled in me an appreciation of movies beyond mere popcorn entertainment.

Special Thanks to:

Nancy Davis, for the technical practicalities of editing any book, but also for having a sixth sense for sending encouraging emails exactly when I needed them.

Brooke Wheeler, for being up at 1 a.m. to answer my little copyediting queries, and for taking on this project with enthusiasm and...dare I say it?...whimsy.

Caroline Parks, for remaining flexible as deadlines shifted and delivering a high-quality index at the right moment.

Liane Thomas, for stepping in at the last minute for some extra copyediting, and turning it around in record time.

Jeff Tolbert, for being a good sport when I needed a model, and for creating the lighting renderings in Chapter 4.

Don Sellers, for getting me up to speed with shooting, lighting, sound, composition, and providing a real-world reference.

Michael Uy at Apple for help early in the project.

Glenn Fleishman, David Blatner, Steve Roth (plus the various long-distance inhabitants) at the Green Lake compound for knowing exactly when to ask, "How's the book coming along?" in addition to everyday comradeship.

Nancy Aldrich-Ruenzel, Connie Jeung-Mills, Gary-Paul Prince, and even some non-hyphenated folks like **Kate Reber, Marjorie Baer, Kim Lombardi, Mimi Heft,** and **Paula Baker** at Peachpit Press.

And, of course, **Kim Carlson,** who never hesitated to ask, "How can I help?" and listened to my ideas about how this book should take shape.

TABLE OF CONTENTS

TABLE OF CONTENTS

INTRODUCTION

When I first heard that Apple was planning to extend video editing to "the rest of us," I was dubious. Despite comparisons with desktop publishing, which brought the world of professional printing to even the most inexperienced publisher, video editing was an entirely different beast. Video has traditionally entailed motion, audio, lighting, and special effects, not to mention the costs of buying or renting a good camera, storing the massive video files on tape or on disk, and then outputting them to a handful of other possible formats. Video editing is a skill that people spend years mastering in specialized schools.

But then Apple introduced iMovie, and seeing it in person at a Macworld Expo was a bonafied "aha" moment for me and most of the people in attendance. *Of course* this was going to work. When Steve Jobs presented a short video of two children playing, I knew the days of long, choppy, unedited videotape recordings was coming to a close. Not only can you easily—let me repeat that: *easily*—capture video footage and transfer it to your computer, you can now edit out all the bad shots, the awkward moments, and those times when the camera was inadvertently left recording while dangling at your side.

INTRODUCTION

Who Should Read This Book

iMovie 2 for Macintosh: Visual QuickStart Guide is aimed at the beginning or intermediate videographer who wants to know how to quickly and easily edit movies in iMovie. Perhaps you've just purchased your first camcorder and want to turn your home movies into little masterpieces, but don't have the time or money to invest in a professional video editing application. Or maybe you're an old hand at shooting video but new to editing the footage on a computer. Then again, maybe you're a budding Spielberg with scripts in your head and a passion for telling stories on film—the movie business is a tough one to crack, but it's entirely possible that your iMovie-edited film could be the springboard for a career in Hollywood. Or you could also be the owner of a new Macintosh, and want to know why Apple is going to the trouble to give you a powerful video editing application *for free*.

Since iMovie's introduction, we've seen a boom in digital video editing. Sure, it was possible before, using much more complicated and expensive programs like Adobe Premiere or After Effects (and you can still take that route). But with iMovie, *anyone* can make a movie. That sounds like the type of hype found in advertisements, I know, but I mean it.

What You Should Know

Every endeavor requires at least some prior knowledge, so I've made some assumptions about your knowledge while writing this book.

◆ **Macintosh fundamentals.** You need to be able to operate your Mac, which includes launching applications, accessing menus, using the mouse, etc. If you're a complete beginner to the Mac, don't worry: play around on the computer for a little while to get a sense of how things work. You'll pick it up quickly, and won't break anything.

◆ **How to use your camcorder.** Although I'll cover some of the basics, this isn't a book about camcorders. You should know how to record, stop, and review what you've recorded.

◆ **How to bounce back after screwing up.** It's inevitable that something won't go the way you wanted it to: a clip got deleted, the wrong transition was applied, you spelled your kids' names wrong in the movie title...you know what I'm talking about. The great thing about iMovie is that you can go back and fix or re-create scenes that didn't turn out as you expected. Have fun with it. I insist.

An iMovie Toolbox

A full-size movie crew can be unbelievably large and take up a city block. You probably won't require that much gear, but a few items are necessary to use iMovie.

◆ **Mac OS 9 or Mac OS X 10.1.** iMovie runs under Apple's now and future operating system, Mac OS X, as well as under Mac OS 9. However, you need a Mac with a PowerPC G3 or G4 processor running at 300 MHz or faster. Apple also says your Mac needs to be equipped with FireWire, but that's not technically true. iMovie will work on a Mac without it, but you lose the capability to directly import footage from your camera.

◆ **iMovie 2.** If you've purchased a Mac matching the specs above, you have iMovie 2 already—look in the folders named *Applications* or *Applications (Mac OS 9)*. If your Mac is older, you can buy iMovie 2 for Mac OS 9 from Apple. See Chapter 6 for how to get iMovie 2.

◆ **A digital camcorder.** This handy and compact device records the raw footage that you will edit in iMovie. If you own a camcorder that's not digital, you can still import video into iMovie using a third-party analog-to-digital converter. That said, I can't stress how much easier it is to work when you have a digital camcorder. See Chapter 7 for details.

◆ **Lots of hard disk space.** Storage is getting cheaper by the day, which is a good thing. You'll need lots. I don't mean a few hundred megabytes tucked away in a corner of your drive. Realistically, if you don't have at least 10 GB (gigabytes) of storage to use for iMovie, shop for a bigger hard drive. See Chapter 7.

The Moviemaking Process

Creating a movie can be a huge spectrum of experience, but for our purposes I'm going to distill it as follows.

1. **Preproduction.** If you're filming a scripted movie (with actors, sets, dialogue, etc.), be sure you hire the actors, build the sets, write the script, and otherwise prepare to shoot a film. See Appendix D for some resources on where to learn more about the process of getting a movie before the cameras. On the other hand, if you're shooting an event or vacation, preproduction may entail making sure you have a camcorder (see Chapter 1), its batteries are charged, and that you have enough tape available.

2. **Capture footage.** With preproduction out of the way, it's time to actually film your movie. The shooting part is when this book starts to come in handy. Chapters 2 through 5 discuss methods of composing your shots, lighting the scenes, and capturing audio.

3. **Import footage into iMovie.** Your tape is full of raw video waiting to be sculpted by your keen eye and innate sense of drama. The next step is importing it onto your computer and into iMovie. See Chapter 7.

4. **Edit your footage in iMovie.** Before iMovie, average folks had no simple way to edit their footage. The result was endless hours of suffering as relatives were forced to watch every outtake, flubbed shot, and those 10 minutes of walking when you thought the camera was turned off. iMovie changes all that. See Chapters 8 through 12 to see how to edit your video and audio, plus add elements such as transitions, titles, and special effects.

5. **Export video.** The movie is complete, and it's a gem. Now you need to share it with the world. Using the information found in Chapters 13, 14, and 15, you can export the movie onto a videotape, as a QuickTime movie for downloading from the Web, or onto a DVD (using Apple's iDVD software).

What You Can Accomplish by the End of this Book

To say, "Prepare your acceptance speech" would be overextending it a bit, but the truth is that you can use iMovie to create a feature film, award-winning documentary, or even just the best darn vacation video you've ever seen. Of course, as you delve deeper into digital video and nonlinear editing (NLE), you'll realize that more options and more control can be had with more sophisticated (and pricey) systems, like Final Cut Pro. But nothing says you can't do what you want with iMovie.

Stepping out of the clouds, you should easily (there's that word again) be able to shoot, edit, and distribute your movie. In the process, you'll find a new respect for film and video—you can't help it. After using iMovie for a few hours, you'll start watching television with a new eye that picks up aspects like pacing, framing, transitions, and audio that you may never have noticed before.

That's been my experience, and now look at me: I've written a book about iMovie. And assembled some of the best darn vacation movies you've ever seen.

Part 1
Shooting

THE DIGITAL CAMCORDER

1

My copy of iMovie sat neglected on my hard drive for months because I had no easy way to import video footage. Sure, I could have used an analog-to-digital converter to bring in the contents of some old videotapes I had lying around (see Chapter 7), but it would have been a hassle. What I needed was a digital camcorder.

Digital camcorders weren't much more than proof-of-concept devices only a few years ago, but the rapid advance of technology has made them plentiful today. Although digital camcorders cost more than analog models, you can still get a good quality one these days for less than $800. You can also easily spend $5,000 or more, with plenty of models falling between those ranges.

For the money, you also get a host of features—and gimmicks. If you've not yet purchased a digital camcorder (and I highly recommend you get one to use with iMovie), this chapter will help you decide which combination of features is right for you. Note that I'll give some examples, but won't be recommending any particular model because (like all technology) the field can change pretty quickly. If you already own a camcorder, give this chapter a quick skim to see which features are important and which you should leave turned off.

Buying a Camcorder

If you don't yet own a digital video (DV) camcorder, you need one. Here's a look at the important characteristics of these devices.

Camcorder size

Shortly before this book was published, Sony announced the Handycam DCR-IP7 in Japan, a digital camcorder that's roughly the same height as a personal digital assistant (PDA) and weighs 11 ounces. For those of us who've had to lug shoulder-mounted VHS cameras, the miniaturization of this technology is amazing. The majority of digital camcorders aren't that small, but they're remarkable nonetheless—many will fit into a large pants pocket (**Figure 1.1**).

The small sizes are ultra convenient, but have two drawbacks. You're paying a premium for compactness, so expect to shell out more money for a smaller device. Also, a small camcorder that doesn't weigh much can be harder to keep steady when shooting. If you're looking for something portable to use for grabbing footage anywhere and anytime, go as small as you can afford. If you anticipate more staged shots, where a camera can sit on a tripod for hours, size becomes less of an issue.

MiniDV tape format

One of the more daunting tasks related to buying a camcorder is sorting through the different tape formats available, but I'm going to make things easy and say: get a camcorder that uses the MiniDV format. MiniDV tapes are compact, store 100 percent digital information, and store between 60 minutes (at SP speed) or 90 minutes (at LP speed) of footage (**Figure 1.2**). They're not particularly cheap, but they aren't too expensive either: I've been able to find 3-packs of MiniDV tapes at electronics stores and online for around $18.

Figure 1.1 Today's digital camcorders are small enough to fit in your palm.

Figure 1.2 As part of the miniaturization of digital camcorders, the tape media is smaller too. But despite the size, MiniDV tapes store roughly an hour of high-quality video.

MiniDV can store roughly 500 horizontal lines of resolution, which means you're capturing more information than other formats (televisions display about 330 lines). It can also record 16-bit audio at 48 kHz, which is slightly better than CD-quality. What's more, MiniDV tapes retain that quality when you record over them, or make copies from other MiniDV tapes. The same can't be said for VHS tapes, which degrade in quality each time you make a copy.

✔ Tips

- Wait...*tape*? Isn't a digital camera supposed to avoid tape altogether? Yes and no. Although the camcorder is capturing footage and storing it digitally, tape is still the dominant—and relatively cheap—medium for storing large quantities of data. In the future, camcorders will probably include small high-density hard disks (like the tiny 5 GB drive used by Apple's iPod), but for now tape is the best solution. The data is still stored as a series of ones and zeros, resulting in better image quality than other tape formats.

- You can also buy 80-minute MiniDV tapes (which record 80 or 120 minutes of footage), but from what I've read, they can be unreliable due to how thin the tape is (which is what makes it possible to put more tape in the same cartridge size). If the tape breaks while filming, you could be looking at an unwelcome repair bill to clean out the camera's recording heads. Frankly, I haven't wanted to risk damaging my camcorder to find out if 80-minute tapes are worth it.

- If you're going on a trip, stock up on MiniDV tapes. It depends where you're vacationing, but I've found you can't find MiniDV tapes everywhere the way you can find VHS tapes. Bring more than you think you'll need.

BUYING A CAMCORDER

FireWire/i.Link

As you'll soon discover, digital video takes up a massive amount of storage space—approximately 3.6 MB *per second* (see Chapter 7). Even a short movie would take forever to transfer from your camcorder to your Mac if it wasn't for the FireWire connection between the two. Also known on Sony camcorders as i.Link, FireWire is necessary to import movies into iMovie (**Figure 1.3**). If the camcorder doesn't include a FireWire port, find another that does.

✔ Tip

- Most digital camcorders don't come with a FireWire cable, even though they include a FireWire port. So when you purchase a camera, be sure to also buy a cable that will bridge the two devices (**Figure 1.4**). It will likely be labeled as an IEEE 1394 (the standard on which FireWire is based) cable, and has a smaller plug on one end. Expect to pay around $30 for this essential add-on.

Number of CCDs

A traditional movie camera records light onto a strip of film as it passes through the lens. In a digital camcorder, the light comes through the lens and is recorded by a charge-coupled device (CCD), containing arrays of thousands or millions of tiny sensors that note what color of light is striking them. When you put the sensors all together, they create the image you see on video. The higher the number of CCDs, the better your image quality is going to be—but it will cost you a pretty penny. Top-of-the-line cameras feature up to 3 CCDs, while consumer-level devices typically only have one.

FireWire port

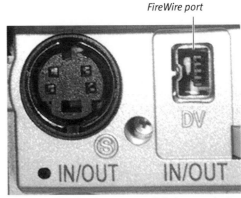

Figure 1.3 The FireWire port on a digital camcorder is smaller than the one on your Mac.

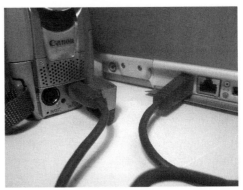

Figure 1.4 Use a high-speed FireWire connection to import your footage into iMovie on your Mac. You'll probably need to purchase a cable like this one, which has both sizes of FireWire plugs.

Figure 1.5 An LCD viewfinder gives you the ability to shoot at odd angles by rotating the screen.

Figure 1.6 Canon's XL1-S is a MiniDV camera with all the trimmings. The microphone is mounted above the unit to record what you're shooting, not the sound of the camera itself.

LCD viewfinder

Most digital camcorders include a liquid crystal display (LCD) viewfinder that pops out from the side of the camera and shows you what the lens sees. LCDs vary in size, from 2.5 inches (diagonal) on up. You can use it in place of the built-in viewfinder, which is often advantageous when you need to hold the camera above your head or near your feet (**Figure 1.5**), or if you're filming yourself and want to make sure your head hasn't slipped out of frame.

The LCD is especially useful when you want to review the footage you've taken, or show some video to a few people looking over your shoulder. And you'll find it invaluable for fast-forwarding to the end of your footage to make sure you don't accidentally shoot over your existing video.

✔ Tip

- Remember that it takes power to light up the LCD's pixels and backlighting. Using it often will drain your camera's batteries faster than using the built-in viewfinder.

Microphone

Every digital camcorder has a microphone, usually built into the body of the camera, but sometimes mounted to the top or front of the camera (**Figure 1.6**). One thing to watch out for is where the microphone is housed: if it's too close to the camcorder's motors, it could pick up the sound of the camera operating (including things like zoom control). Whenever possible, experiment with a few different camcorder models to see what their audio output is like. You can also attach an external microphone to the camera. See Chapter 5 for more information.

Electronic image stabilization

It's likely that I'll spend this entire book saying, "You know what else is great about digital?" So I'll help you get used to it now. Another great thing about a modern digital camcorder is that the software running it can help you stabilize your image and prevent the shaky footage associated with small handheld cameras. To do this, the camcorder uses an outer portion of the total image as reference, then compares movement of objects within the field of view to the outer area (**Figure 1.7**). If most of the image moves together, the software assumes that the whole camera is moving instead of just the objects, and compensates by shifting the active image.

Electronic image stabilization is helpful, but certainly has its drawbacks. It doesn't record the entire screen, so in some cases you may find that objects on the periphery don't wind up in the final footage. It's also not good if you're intentionally moving the camera, such as when you pan or zoom, because the software has to figure out that your motion is deliberate; the end result is sometimes blurry motion that would otherwise be clearer. Still, compared to footage that looks like it was shot during an earthquake, these trade-offs become more acceptable.

Guide area   *Reference*

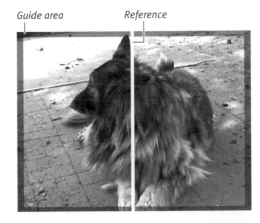

Image shifted   *Reference shifted*

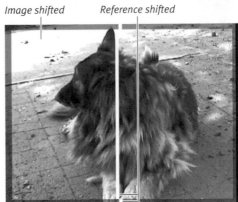

Figure 1.7 In this massively simplified diagram, the original image (top) is shifted to the left by the camera operator's nervousness around such an obviously vicious animal. The camera compares the image to the pixels in the unrecorded guide area (bottom) and compensates by shifting the main image to match. (The reference line shown here is purely for this explanation—the camera doesn't actually have a line running through the middle of the image. Instead, it divides the image into several quadrants and continually compares the guide area to the image area.)

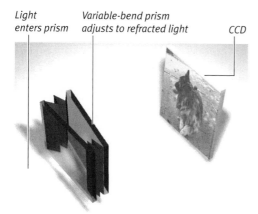

Light enters prism
Variable-bend prism adjusts to refracted light
CCD

Figure 1.8 An optical image stabilization system uses two lenses to detect light refraction.

Optical image stabilization

Another option for stabilizing your video is to buy a camera with optical image stabilization. Unlike the digital method, optical stabilization uses a prism composed of two lenses with silicon fluid between them. The prism determines whether the light coming into the lens is refracted (think of looking through a water's surface at a straight stick and how it appears to bend). If it is, the camcorder adjusts the lenses to remove the refraction (**Figure 1.8**). An optical stabilizer can work a bit slower than electronic stabilization—since it's performing mechanical, not digital, adjustments—but tends to be a bit smoother overall.

Lens optics

The camera's lens is your eye to the footage you'll shoot, so optical quality is an important consideration. All of the lenses are good, but more-expensive models tend to feature better optics.

Remote control

It's not like you have enough remote controls lying around the house. I thought having a remote control for a camera was a dumb idea until I realized its two main purposes: playing back video when the camera is attached to a television or monitor, and controlling recording when you can't be near the camera (such as when you're in the frame). The remote ended up being more important than I thought.

BUYING A CAMCORDER

Features Worth Noting

Electronics manufacturers love to make bulleted lists of features. Some you may never need or want, while others can help you improve the footage you shoot.

Focus

It's a safe bet that you want the subjects in your video to be in focus—but which subjects, and when? Camcorders feature automatic focus control, which is great when you're shooting footage on the fly. Who wants to try to manually focus when following an eagle in flight (**Figure 1.9**)?

However, sometimes the automatic focus can be too good, bringing most objects in a scene into focus—which is why camcorders include an option for manually focusing the lens. (Higher-end models include a focus ring built around the lens, like on a 35mm still camera. Most smaller camcorders sport small dials or scroll wheels to control manual focus.) Manual focus is essential for some situations, such as interviews, when you're not moving the camera (see Chapter 2).

Shutter speed

The term "shutter speed" is a bit misleading here, since a digital camcorder doesn't technically have a shutter (a door or iris that opens quickly to allow light to enter the lens). However, it's possible to duplicate the effects of different shutter speeds by changing the setting on the camera. This is good for filming action with movement that would otherwise appear blurry (such as sporting events). Shutter speed is measured in fractions of a second, so a setting of 1/60 is slower than 1/8000 (see Chapter 2).

Figure 1.9 Gratuitous vacation footage inserted here. But really, when you're shooting video on the run, trying to manually focus at the same time would have meant losing the shot. You can view this movie clip at the *iMovie VQS* companion Web site (www.peachpit.com/vqs/imovie/).

Normal

Low-light setting

Figure 1.10 Some camcorders feature a low-light setting, which boosts the effectiveness of the available light.

S-Video port

Figure 1.11 An S-Video port offers higher-quality image playback on televisions and monitors.

Night vision/low light

You have a few options for filming in low-light conditions. You could always carry around a full lighting setup, but that's not realistic. To compensate, some cameras include a night-vision mode that picks up heat from objects near the camera and displays a greenish representation of the scene.

Other cameras may include a low-light setting, which boosts the amount of available light that's picked up by the camera's image sensors (**Figure 1.10**). It's surprisingly effective, though the playback tends to be stuttered or blurry if there's a lot of movement in the scene.

S-Video port

All camcorders offer some type of output port so you can hook up a television or monitor to play back your footage. Usually, RCA-style plugs are included, but some models also offer an S-Video port (**Figure 1.11**). Hooking up a TV with an S-Video cable gives a clearer picture than the other AV cables. Use it if you've got it.

FEATURES WORTH NOTING

Features to Ignore/Avoid

Just as there are features you should pay attention to, some features should be ignored or outright avoided. Most of these are included for buyers who don't have the means to edit their movies after shooting. But iMovie does all of the following better than a camera. Most importantly, these effects permanently alter your footage, which you can't correct later in iMovie.

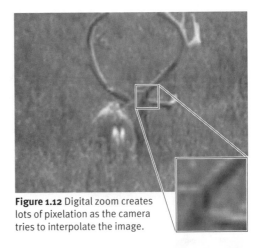

Figure 1.12 Digital zoom creates lots of pixelation as the camera tries to interpolate the image.

◆ **Digital zoom.** One of the first features you'll see on a camera is that it has a 200x (or higher) digital zoom. The technical interpretation is that the computer inside the camera digitally enlarges the image it's seeing and appears as if the camera is zoomed beyond its optical capabilities (**Figure 1.12**). The real-world interpretation, at least for now, is that some marketer somewhere is smiling and thinking about the wisdom of P.T. Barnum. Digital zoom isn't pure hokum, but it's also not a mature enough technology to be used in your movies. I expect that as cameras become more powerful and the image processing chips and software speed up (as they inevitably will), digital zoom will become a powerful tool. But not yet.

◆ **Special effects.** Before iMovie, you couldn't apply "sophisticated" techniques like fade-in or fade-out without using an expensive professional editing system. So, camcorder makers added the capability to apply fades, wipes, and image distortions like sepia tones or solarization (**Figure 1.13**). Well, forget special effects entirely—you can do them better in iMovie, with more control, and without degrading your footage.

Figure 1.13 In-camera special effects are really only good for ruining otherwise good footage. And not to sound mean, but the Mosaic (top) and Art (bottom) effects shown here aren't even that interesting. Let iMovie handle your effects (see Chapter 12).

Date stamp

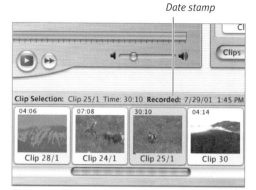

Figure 1.14 iMovie displays the date and time a clip was shot, so you don't need to use a date stamp feature that permanently adds it to the footage.

◆ **Date stamp.** You can optionally display the date and time on your footage, which would appear to be helpful if not for the fact that the information remains on the tape. Even with this feature disabled, your camcorder is recording (but not displaying) this information, which shows up in iMovie when you select a clip (**Figure 1.14**). Similarly, avoid built-in title generators.

◆ **Still photo.** Some entry-level camcorders advertise the capability to take still photos, but it's a bit of a ruse. In reality, the camera is taking a still picture and writing it to about 5 seconds of tape (since it's still recording during that time, you'll get five seconds of audio, even when the image is unchanged). Again, iMovie can do this better without wasting tape by creating a still clip from a single frame of video (see Chapter 8). But another problem is that the photos are stored at video resolution, which is 72 dots per inch (dpi) and interlaced (every other line is displayed on a television screen).

Check your camera for details. Some more expensive cameras now have the capability to keep still photos separate. They capture progressive-scan images, which means every pixel is grabbed, and then save them to a separate memory card (such as MultiMedia Card or Sony Memory Stick cards).

COMPOSITION & COVERAGE   2

Camcorder in hand, it's time to start shooting. Where to start? The easiest route is to point the lens at something and start recording. You're bound to get some good footage. However, by learning how to improve your video when you shoot it, you'll end up with better source footage when it's time to edit.

The material in this chapter (and the rest of the chapters in this section of the book) isn't rocket science. If you've grown up watching television or movies (as we all have, to varying degrees), some of it may be too obvious to warrant mentioning. And yet, when it comes time to shoot, it's all too easy to forget the basics and just let the camcorder run—again, perfectly acceptable, but you might kick yourself when you start working with your footage in iMovie. Remember, with iMovie you can edit your clips into a professional-looking movie, but it can't help you improve mediocre source material.

In this chapter, I'll touch upon the basics of getting a shot, and introduce you to some techniques for framing your scenes and shooting plenty of coverage to work with later. Depending on what you're shooting, some or all of this material may apply—you may have control over aspects such as lighting and how the subjects act, or you may be on safari trying to videotape elephants while avoiding getting eaten by lions.

Preproduction

In general, the term preproduction refers to everything done before the camera starts rolling. I think it's safe to assume that you know how to operate your camcorder, and you probably know roughly what you want to shoot. The following steps—except for the first one, which I consider essential—are optional, depending on the type of movie you're shooting (for example, feel free to storyboard your baby's first steps, but she'll ultimately be the one to decide how that scene plays out).

◆ **Imagine the End Result.** Before you even turn on your camcorder's power, start with an idea of what type of video you'll end up with. Will it be viewed on a television, movie screen, computer monitor, or maybe a combination of each? This decision will help you when shooting. For example, if your movie will only appear on the Web, you may want to shoot more close-ups of people, to make sure they're identifiable in a 320 by 160-pixel window on your computer screen. If it's going to be shown on a big-screen television, on the other hand, you could frame your shots with wider vistas or complex background action in the shot.

◆ **Write the script.** If you're shooting a fictional story, with scenes, sets, actors, and the like, you're going to need a script. I know, the bigwigs in Hollywood don't always start movies with a script, but you've no doubt seen one of those stinkers and wondered if entire sections of Los Angeles underwent covert lobotomies. A good movie starts with a good script, without exception. Even in the low-budget world of digital video filmmaking, a good script can often overcome bland direction, lighting, staging, acting, sound, etc.

An Afternoon, A Life

Shortly after starting work on this book, I spent an afternoon with a colleague of mine, who also happens to be an Emmy-winning filmmaker, to pick his brain about filmmaking. "Anything in particular?" he asked me.

"Shooting, lighting, sound...," I replied.

He laughed. "Some people," he said, "spend their entire lives learning just one of those skills."

Filmmaking is an evolutionary art, and involves far more than I can include in this book. I'll cover the basics, but I highly recommend consulting Appendix D for resources on where to learn more about shooting.

Figure 2.1 Drawing up a storyboard will help you visualize your shots and save time. If you're shooting casually or on the go, create a list of shots you want to try to get.

◆ **Create storyboards.** Another step in producing a good fictional movie is creating storyboards: shot-by-shot sketches of what you want to shoot (**Figure 2.1**). In fact, you can use storyboards for documentary-style shooting, too. The point of storyboarding is to formulate your idea of what to shoot before you actually shoot; this process will save you time and help ensure that you're capturing all the visuals you want. At the very least, make a list of things you want to shoot, even if you're grabbing vacation video.

◆ **Prepare your equipment.** Do you have plenty of MiniDV cassettes? Spare batteries (and are they charged)? Lens cleaning cloth? Tripod? "Going to shoot video" can simply mean bringing your body and camcorder; or it can involve hauling truckloads of equipment. In either case, make sure you have what you'll need to accomplish the job.

PREPRODUCTION

Understanding Time Code

As you shoot, you're recording video to the MiniDV tape. If you ever want to find that footage again, you need to understand time code, the method all camcorders use to label and keep track of footage. You'll use time code constantly in iMovie, to the point where it becomes as natural as breathing.

As the tape advances, the camcorder notes where footage is being recorded and displays it in the viewfinder or on the LCD screen (**Figure 2.2**). A full time code notation looks like this:

   01:42:38:12

The interpretation of those numbers is a lot like telling time on a digital clock, except for the last two digits:

   Hours:Minutes:Seconds:Frames

So our time code number above is read as 1 hour, 42 minutes, 38 seconds, and 12 frames. Digital video records at 30 frames per second, so the last number starts at :00 and ends at :29.

When you're recording, you typically won't see all of those numbers. Something like 0:03:31 (zero hours, 3 minutes, and 31 seconds) is more common, because the camera doesn't split out partial seconds (so no frame numbers are shown). In iMovie, however, you can split clips between frames, not just between seconds, so the full number becomes important (see Chapter 8).

Time code indicator

Figure 2.2 The camera assigns a time code to each frame of film, which is used to manage your footage later in iMovie.

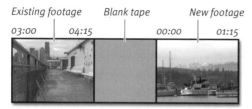

Existing footage   *Blank tape*   *New footage*

03:00   04:15   00:00   01:15

Figure 2.3 Broken time code occurs when blank tape exists between your footage. The camcorder uses the last known time code marker (in this example, 04:15) to compute the time for later frames. However, the portion of blank tape before the new footage has reset the time code back to zero (00:00).

Keeping Time Code Intact

The camcorder's time code indicator ticks away as you shoot, so in theory you can reach the end of a 60-minute tape with a time code value of 59:59:29 (or thereabouts; I don't think I've ever actually wrapped up a tape that was exactly 60 minutes in length).

However, depending on how you've been shooting, you may notice that the time code has started over at zero at some point. If this happens, your time code is broken.

Before you complain to the manufacturer, look at how you were shooting. If you rewound the tape to review some footage, then started again a few seconds after the end of that clip, you inadvertently broke the time code. The camera counts forward based on the last time code recorded. If you move into an area of tape that hasn't been marked with a time code, the camera doesn't know where to begin counting, and starts over at zero (**Figure 2.3**). Fortunately, there's a way to fix broken time code as you're shooting—but you'll record over any video recoded after the breaking point.

To fix broken time code:

1. With your camera in Play (VCR) mode, rewind the tape until you see the last footage with unbroken time code.

2. Advance the tape until you're about two seconds from the end of that footage.

3. Switch the camcorder to Camera mode and begin recording from that point.

continues on next page

UNDERSTANDING TIME CODE

✔ Tips

- iMovie doesn't use time code to work with the tape in your camera. Most high-end video editing packages let you specify a time code value and then the program advances or rewinds the tape to that point. In iMovie, that task is up to you. If you have unbroken time code on your tape, it's a lot easier for you to find the footage you're looking for without having to review every minute.

- Maintaining unbroken time code means less wear and tear on your camera. When you search by reviewing your footage, the tape is in contact with the playhead inside the camera. A camcorder's life span is based on the number of hours the play-head is used, so repeatedly scanning the video using the fast-forward and rewind features while it's playing contributes to the wear of the playhead. Instead, forward or rewind the cassette without playing it, when the tape is not in contact with the playhead. This doesn't mean you're going to kill the camera by viewing your foot-age, just that you are helping to speed the process a little.

I Broke It. So What?

It's not essential that you maintain unbro-ken time code throughout your video. Such breaks aren't going to damage your footage, or even confuse iMovie. They will make it more difficult for you to go back and locate specific scenes that you've shot, however. It's far easier to insert your tape and advance to 0:27:18 than to remember that your scene is at 0:02:24 somewhere in the middle of the tape.

Shooting Video Without Disruption

I'm always a little self-conscious when I'm shooting, because often I have to make myself conspicuous in order to get the shot I want. On vacation, this isn't always a problem (my little camcorder is much less intrusive than that other guy's honkin' 35mm lens), but some occasions—for example, weddings—call for discretion. There are a few different approaches to shooting without disruption.

For one, you don't have to shoot with the camera in front of your face. You can rotate the LCD screen and film from your hip (or even shoot behind you). If it's inevitable that your camera is going to be noticeable, don't be rude about it. People will understand if you need to step softly into view for a few seconds to get a shot, then retreat to a neutral location. Depending on the circumstances, try to ingratiate yourself into the scene so the people involved will trust that you won't be obnoxious.

Or, you could take the route of a professional still photographer who was on a recent vacation I took: not only was he taking great pictures, he offered to sell the resulting photo album to fellow vacationers. People (at least the ones I assume who paid) no longer seemed to mind so much if he blocked their view.

Take Notes

When you're shooting, you may think you'll remember that the panda bears were located at roughly the 24-minute mark of the tan Panasonic tape, but in reality you'll find yourself scanning through the footage and wishing you'd taken the time to take notes. Get a simple binder and make columns for the tape, time code, and notes. Then as you're shooting, jot down what you've just filmed. It doesn't have to be complicated, as long as it offers a quick reference to where your scenes occur. Taking notes is also essential when you need to keep track of locations and the names of people who appear in your video.

✔ Tips

■ Label your tapes. They add up quickly, tend to look alike, and are guaranteed to fall off your desk in a cluttered heap just before you need to grab the right one in a hurry.

■ I hate taking notes, too. With digital video, however, you have an advantage: before or after a shot, simply keep the camera running and speak your details. It won't help you find a clip in the middle of a tape, but it will give you the important details of what was recorded.

Composing Your Shots

If you really want to, you can hold the camcorder up in the air and hit record—with your eyes closed. But putting a small amount of thought into the composition of your shots, you can give them a much more professional look.

Shoot large

I had the opportunity to see a 70mm print of *Lawrence of Arabia* a few years ago on the massive screen at Seattle's Cinerama theater. The movie is filled with sweeping desert vistas where you can see miles in every direction, taking full advantage of a large-screen experience.

Most likely, your video will instead play on a television screen or as a QuickTime movie on a Web page (**Figure 2.4**). For that reason, try to "shoot large"—make sure the subject is large enough in the frame that it's instantly recognizable even on a small screen. Getting closer also reveals more detail than can be seen from a distance.

Maintain an axis

Most people are fluent enough in the language of film that they aren't thrown by sudden cuts or changes in a scene. But crossing an axis tends to freak them out. The idea is this: if you have two people in a scene, and you're switching between close-ups of each one, they should both remain on their own sides of the screen (**Figure 2.5**). If character A is on the left side of the table, but then you move the camera so that he appears on the right side of the *screen*, the viewer is left wondering how he moved so quickly. At the very least, she'll notice that something odd has happened, which distracts her from the movie's content.

Figure 2.4 Sweeping vistas don't always work in small movie windows, so try to shoot large when you can. Don't abandon them, however. Tape is relatively cheap, so grab the shot when it's available; you can intercut the wider shots later when you're editing in iMovie. See "Coverage" later in this chapter.

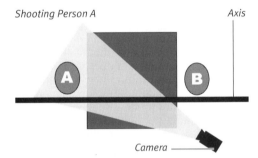
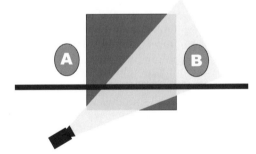

Figure 2.5 Keeping the camera on the same side of your axis line helps the viewer maintain a mental geography of the scene.

Figure 2.6 The train's engine appears in the first third vertical portion of this shot.

Figure 2.7 When your subject faces into the frame, he remains engaged with the rest of the shot, rather than looking outside the frame at something else (which is where your viewers will want to look in that case).

Balance your shots

As I look through still photos I've taken over the years, I notice an annoying consistency: everything is centered. People, monuments, sunsets—all evenly positioned between the edges of the frame. Perhaps it's just our nature to center objects, but it's a good habit to break. Go watch a movie or television and you'll see that almost nothing is centered.

Positioning elements slightly askew of center makes them more interesting. Another take on this positioning is called the rule of thirds: the focus of your composition should appear one third of the way from the edge of the frame (**Figure 2.6**). When you do, also make sure that the subject is facing into the frame, not toward the outside (**Figure 2.7**).

✔ Tips

- As you're shooting, be aware of everything in your field of view—don't just focus your attention on the subject. If something else is distracting or disturbing elsewhere in the frame, viewers will likely gravitate toward that, and away from your subject.

- Similarly, take your environment into consideration when possible. Because video is interlaced (every other horizontal line on the screen is displayed), some objects such as window blinds may create distracting patterns onscreen.

- Many cameras today have the capability to shoot in a 16:9 aspect ratio, also known as widescreen mode. On the camera, it looks as if the image has been squished in from the sides, but some video editing programs can interpret the ratio correctly. Unfortunately, iMovie is not one of those programs. Video shot in 16:9 remains squished in iMovie.

Focus

Pity the poor UFO watchers of days gone by, with their bulky cameras and—most distressingly—manual focus. It's hard enough to spot a saucer in the sky, but to also keep it in clear focus was a daunting task.

I suspect that today's sky-watchers are thrilled with modern camcorders, if for no other reason than the inclusion of *automatic focus control*. Thanks to millions of calculations processed while shooting, a camcorder can do an amazing job of keeping objects in focus. Sometimes, however, the camera performs its job too well.

Automatic focus versus manual focus

Digital camcorders use automatic focus by default. Although they include some sort of manual focus control (which is often a small dial that's hard to adjust in the middle of shooting), most likely it's not the type of focus ring found on your 35mm still camera. Nonetheless, don't be tempted to let automatic focus dominate your shots.

Auto focus tends to focus everything in view, causing footage to appear hyper-real at times (**Figure 2.8**). Your eyes don't bring everything into focus as you look around, so video that is predominantly focused can be distracting.

In an ironic twist, automatic focus can actually contribute to blurry images. The camera generally attempts to focus the objects in the foreground (which may appear on the periphery of the image and not be immediately visible to you), but that can throw off the focus in the rest of the shot and leave your subjects blurry (**Figure 2.9**).

If your camera is mostly stationary, experiment with manual focus to make sure the objects you want to be in focus remain in focus.

Figure 2.8 Camcorders do a good job of focusing—sometimes too good. In this shot, Greta is competing with the chair and the firepit in the background for the viewer's attention.

Figure 2.9 Objects in the foreground can throw off your camcorder's automatic focus.

Focus

Figure 2.10 The background is out of focus and lit dimly compared to the foreground, helping to visually separate the two.

Depth of Field

We usually want to keep things in focus, but when everything appears sharp, most scenes begin to look flat. Instead, highlight objects in the foreground by keeping them in focus, and separate them from the background by keeping it soft. When you increase this depth of field, you're more effectively simulating how a viewer's vision works, and subtly influencing what should be seen. This works particularly well during interviews or scenes where a character is occupying the frame.

To increase depth of field:

1. Position the camera as far away from your subject as possible.

2. Use the camcorder's zooming controls to zoom in close to the subject.

3. Set the manual focus so that the subject is clear (**Figure 2.10**).

✔ Tip

- If you're shooting a fixed object where the camera won't move (such as a person being interviewed), use manual focus. Sometimes the motion of the person talking (if they move forward slightly when making a point, for example) will trigger the camera to adjust its focus, causing other elements in the frame to "bounce."

DEPTH OF FIELD

25

Coverage

With some basics under your belt about framing your shots, we come to a bigger question: what shots are needed to create a movie? If you're shooting a family event, you may think the question doesn't apply to you; after all, you shoot whatever happens, right?

Well, shooting the event itself is a good start, but you need more than that. And you need to make sure you have enough *coverage*, the footage that will give you plenty of room to work when you're editing in iMovie.

Shoot to edit

At the beginning of this chapter, I advised you to imagine the end result of your movie before you begin shooting. A similar notion is shooting to edit. In the days before anyone with a Mac could edit their movies, amateur filmmakers shot "in the camera," meaning they structured their shot process so that scenes fell sequentially in the order they would appear when the tape was played— "editing" was done in advance by planning what to shoot.

Instead, you're shooting with the knowledge that your raw footage is going to be edited in iMovie. You don't have to shoot things in order, limit yourself to the main subject, or even use footage from the same session.

By way of example, suppose you're filming a family reunion. Immediately following the pick-up basketball game (where Uncle Barney surprised everyone with 32 points and a slam dunk), you shoot a few minutes of a woodpecker perched on a nearby tree. Then you return to the festivities. The woodpecker has nothing to do with the family reunion, so you may not even use it in your final video—or perhaps you'll pop a few seconds of it into the beginning to show what a beautiful, nature-filled location everyone enjoyed.

Figure 2.11 An establishing shot gives the viewer a sense of where the scene is beginning, such as this shot of the entrance to a location where the next scenes will occur.

As another example, to round out your movie you want to show the sunset and then fade to black. Unfortunately, the sunset footage you shot wasn't as memorable as you remembered, so instead you grab 20 seconds of sunset footage you took on another location and insert that into your movie. Unless it's painfully obvious that the two locations are different (the presence of a sandy beach where before you were in the middle of a forest, for example), no one will know the difference, and your movie will end stronger. In each example, you had extra footage at your disposal because you were shooting to edit.

Types of coverage

When shooting a feature-length motion picture, a director will use multiple camera setups to shoot as much coverage as possible. So in one scene, the camera may shoot both actors in the frame, each actor from one or more different positions, and various combinations of points of view. The goal is to present a scene in the edited movie where the camera position is integral to the scene's mood or content.

◆ **Establishing shot.** This is usually an overview shot that's wide enough to let the viewer know the setting and which characters inhabit the scene (**Figure 2.11**). It can be a sign reading "Welcome to Twin Falls," a shot of someone's house, or a shot of a room. The important thing is that the establishing shot provides a physical geography of where objects appear. (This technique is used to great effect in dozens of movies and television shows: you see an establishing shot of the Chicago skyline and assume that the action takes place there, even though the actual filming took place in Vancouver.)

continues on next page

COVERAGE

◆ **Medium shot.** Most shots end up as variations of medium shots. Generally, this shot is large enough to frame two or three people's torsos, although it can vary between a shot of a single person or half of a room (**Figure 2.12**).

◆ **Close-up.** The screen is filled with part of a person or object (**Figure 2.13**). Close-ups usually show a person's head and shoulders, but can also push in closer (known as an extreme close-up) so you see only the person's eyes. Other examples of close-ups include shots of a person's hands, or any object that occupies the entire frame.

◆ **Cut-away shots.** Sometimes referred to as B-roll footage, cut-aways are shots of associated objects or scenes that aren't necessarily part of the central action in a scene. An example would be the view from a ship traveling through a passage, which cuts away to a shot of the darkening sky, then returns to the ship safely emerging from the passage. The woodpecker footage mentioned in the family reunion example could easily be used as a cut-away shot.

◆ **In points and out points.** If possible, give yourself some shots that can be used to enter or exit a scene, sometimes known as in points and out points. For example, if you're shooting an interview and your subject has just declared his intention to walk on Mars, don't immediately stop recording. Hold the camera on him as he finishes speaking, then perhaps pan down to his desk where a model of his rocket ship is mounted.

Figure 2.12 A medium shot is typically close enough to include two or three people.

Figure 2.13 A close-up focuses on one person or object that occupies most of the frame.

✔ Tips

- Linger on shots when you can. It's far easier to cut footage out than to add it back in later (especially if it's vacation footage or something similar...unless you *really* need to rationalize a trip back!)

- How long should you hold on to a shot? First of all, don't automatically shut off the camcorder right when the action has stopped. Linger for a few seconds or minutes to let the emotion of a scene dissipate. This is true when you're doing interviews or shooting wildlife. You can always trim it later in iMovie.

- Here's a tip I came across while on a soggy camping trip. When shooting in poor weather, you'll need to protect your gear. You can buy hoods and covers and other accessories, which are fine but add bulk. Instead, I have a fleece vest that I use to cover the camera: the lens points through one arm hole, protecting it from the rain but still giving enough room to operate the camera.

THE CAMERA IN MOTION

3

My digital camcorder is small enough that I can take it almost anywhere. While we're driving to work, my wife will occasionally grab the camera out of my bag and start shooting anything that catches her eye: a brilliant sunrise, the way Seattle's skyline materializes on a foggy morning, rows of orange-tipped trees alongside the freeway in the fall. Although we initially bought the camera to take with us on vacation, it has turned into an unofficial chronicler of our lives right now.

One of the advantages of a small camera is that it easily moves with you. However, when you're shooting, motion can become a character in its own right. Slowly moving across a scene imparts a different feeling than quickly scanning your surroundings, for example. This chapter addresses the most common ways of moving the camera to add motion to your movie, including the number one rule: don't move.

Don't Move

It's time to go watch TV again (hey, this moviemaking stuff is easy!). Turn to a scripted dramatic show and note how often the camera moves. I don't mean how often the *camera is moved*, which provides different angles of the same scene, but how often the camera is actually moving—not much. When it does move, such as when following a character through a set (*The West Wing* often uses this technique when transitioning between scenes), the movement is smooth and measured.

As much as possible, limit your camera's movement. You want action that moves the viewer, which is more likely to happen when the camera is stationary and focused on the contents of a scene. A shot that's bouncing, zooming, or otherwise sloshing about like a drunk at happy hour is a scene where the movement is distracting from the action. Of course, there are times when motion is called for: can you imagine reality-television shows like *COPS* using stationary cameras? I imagine it's difficult enough to chase a suspected criminal down a dark alley and over a chain-link fence without asking him to pause for a few minutes while the crew sets up its lights and tripods.

Staying still has another practical benefit: excess movement causes blurring in your images (**Figure 3.1**). Our eyes do a good job of pulling detail out of motion blur, but there's a limit to how often they can tolerate fuzzy swabs of color streaking across the screen.

Figure 3.1 Sudden camera moves introduce blurriness to your footage. Try to keep the camera stationary for most of your shots, if possible.

Figure 3.2 Optical zoom and automatic focus can be a great combination when you're shooting something from far away.

Start with the camera zoomed out...

...and slowly zoom in...

...then hold on the zoomed-in image before slowly zooming back out.

Figure 3.3 Quick zooms in and out are effective ways to instill headaches in your viewers. Instead, slowly zoom in, hold, then slowly zoom out. This technique gives you good clear footage at several distances.

Zooming

Now that I've lectured on the evils of moving your camera, let's get into the realities of the types of motion you'll encounter. To start, let's look at one of the most common troublemakers, the zoom control.

When you bought your camera, the first thing you probably did was play with the zoom control. It's usually a rocker switch that moves between W (wide) and T (telephoto), and enables you to view distant objects. Combined with a camera's automatic focus feature, especially when shooting in the field, zooming can get you closer to your subject (**Figure 3.2**).

However, the control can be sensitive, leading to abrupt or too-quick zooms in and out. A better approach is to smoothly zoom in on your subject, hold for a bit, then slowly zoom out (**Figure 3.3**). Practice with the control to get a feel for how much pressure is needed, and try to run through the shot a few times before you actually record it.

✔ Tips

- If you missed the memo in Chapter 1: turn off the digital zoom feature of your camera. The camera tries to enlarge the pixels, thereby appearing to zoom beyond its optical limit. All you really end up with is large blocky pixels.

- Sometimes you want an abrupt zoom, either because it enhances the action or because you don't have time to shoot, stop recording, zoom in, then begin recording again. In the latter case, zoom quickly and hold onto the shot—you can edit out the actual zoom later in iMovie.

- A good zoom is handy when you're not recording. If you're not toting a pair of binoculars, your camcorder will help you see objects in the distance.

Dollying

Dollying is similar to zooming, in that the camera moves in toward (or away from) a subject. However, a dolly shot doesn't use the zoom control at all. In feature film shoots, a dolly is a platform that holds the camera and rides on rails similar to railroad tracks. When filming, one or more people (known as grips) push the dolly, resulting in a smooth shot.

When you zoom, the camcorder's lens is simulating the appearance of moving closer to your subject. When dollying, you're actually moving the camera closer. The difference is especially pronounced in the background, which appears different depending on the method you use (**Figure 3.4**).

✔ Tips

- As with zooming, you want to ease in and out of a dolly shot. Grips aren't just people who push equipment around. A good grip can accelerate and decelerate smoothly and, often more importantly, *consistently* during multiple takes.

- A dolly shot is a professional-looking camera move, but it's likely you don't have a dolly setup or want to spend the money to rent one. But you can use a number of alternative dollies. Wheelchairs are great (and comfortable!), and skateboards also work in a pinch. It doesn't matter so much how you get the shot, only that the shot turns out the way you want it.

Zoomed in

Pushed in on dolly, no zoom

Figure 3.4 These two shots are similarly framed, but look at the plant in the background to see how the two approaches differ.

DOLLYING

Automatic

1/8000 shutter speed   *Uncorrected brightness*

Figure 3.5 A higher shutter speed can make fast-moving objects appear clearer. However, it also requires more light—I had to boost the brightness of the bottom image in an image editor to make it easier to see (original is on the right).

Changing Shutter Speed

Your camcorder doesn't have a shutter in the traditional sense. There's no little door that opens and closes quickly to control the amount of light that gets through the lens. However, camcorders can simulate shutter speed by controlling how quickly the CCD sensors refresh the image being recorded, which is measured in times per second. A normal shutter speed is approximately 1/60th of a second, meaning the CCD samples an image 60 times per second.

Why change shutter speed? Using a higher setting is good for capturing fast-moving action like sporting events. The blur caused by moving objects is substantially reduced at speeds of 1/4000 or 1/8000, creating frames that contain very little blurring (**Figure 3.5**). You'll need to experiment with your camera's settings, though; a high shutter speed can also make the image appear to strobe, or flash artificially.

✔ Tips

- Faster shutter speeds require more light. If you think of a traditional shutter, not as much light enters the camera when the shutter is closing more times per second. So a dimly lit room can appear even darker at a high shutter speed.

- Your camcorder is probably changing shutter speeds without your knowledge. On Auto setting, it detects what kind of light is present, and if it detects fluorescent lighting—which flickers imperceptibly to our eyes, but can cause havoc on a digital recording—the shutter speed automatically changes to compensate.

Panning

Film has the great advantage of width: its wider aspect ratio captures landscape images in a way your video camcorder can only dream. However, you can pivot the camera left or right to shoot that landscape and not disrupt the scene with too much motion. This side-to-side movement is called panning, and is a common tool in a director's box of shots. A similar shot, tilting, moves the camera up and down, though it's not used as frequently.

To pan a scene:

1. Set your camera up on a tripod for best results, or hold it as steady as you can.

2. Determine where the pan will begin and end.

3. Begin recording at the first point, and pivot the camera left or right at an even pace. If it's not mounted on a tripod, swivel your body at the hips.

4. When you reach the end point of your pan, stop recording.

Pan ahead of subjects

A panning shot often follows a subject from one side of the screen to the other, but think of your composition as you do this. Don't just center the subject in the frame. Instead, provide space into which the person can walk by panning ahead of him (**Figure 3.6**).

Figure 3.6 Frame your shots so that subjects walk into the shot when panning, not out the edges.

Figure 3.7 It's either you or the camera—the world just doesn't naturally tip like that.

✔ Tips

- To help stabilize the camera while you're holding it, pull your elbows in close to your body, hold the camera with both hands, and keep a wide stance.

- If you're using a tripod, be sure to get a fluid-head tripod. It's more expensive than your standard unit, but allows for much smoother motion.

- As it turns out, the biggest problem with panning isn't moving the camera smoothly. Your number one concern should be: is the horizon level? If the camera isn't exactly even with the horizon, panning will give the effect of moving uphill or downhill (**Figure 3.7**).

- Panning doesn't have to involve rotating the camera around a central axis. Use a dolly (see "Dollying," earlier) setup to move the camera from side to side.

LIGHTING

4

Unless you plan to shoot with the lens cap on, you'll have to come to grips with lighting in your videos. Put simply, you want to have enough light to see what's being filmed, but not so much that it blows out the camcorder's sensors with pure white. You also don't want scenes that are so dark you can't see what's going on.

When a Hollywood film crew shoots a movie, the lighting you see is enhanced (or outright artificial—even the most natural-looking sunlight coming through a window is likely a big spotlight on the other side of the wall). You don't need to go to those extremes, of course. Most often your lighting rigs will entail the sun, some lamps, and maybe a spotlight or two.

What's important is that you know how basic lighting works, and how to take advantage of it to ensure that the objects you're shooting don't show up as dark talking blobs when you're editing.

Hard and Soft Light

There are infinite possible combinations of light, which can seem daunting when you're shooting video. Fortunately, for our purposes we can break light down into two broad categories: hard and soft.

◆ **Hard light.** The term hard light refers to the light produced by a direct source, which creates shadows with clearly defined edges (**Figure 4.1**). Hard light tends to be bright, like the sun at midday.

◆ **Soft light.** In contrast, soft light isn't as direct, and produces shadows that are blurred at the edges or fade away (**Figure 4.2**). Soft light is typically light that's filtered by artificial means (such as hoods and filters attached to the light) or by natural means (such as clouds, fog, or shade).

In general, soft light is better to film, because it gives you more levels of brightness and accentuates natural textures. Hard light creates a lot of contrast, limiting the brightness levels because you see either high-intensity light or deep, dark shadows.

✔ Tip

■ If lighting is particularly important to a scene, add a video monitor to your list of equipment to bring on a video shoot. Although your camcorder offers a viewfinder and an LCD, you won't know how the image will look on a TV screen until you see it projected on a monitor. The camera's LCD is great for viewing the content you're capturing, but LCDs can often display images brighter than they're being recorded; or, if you're outside, the LCD's pixels can get washed out by the sunlight.

Figure 4.1 Hard light creates sharp, clearly defined shadows. A bright halogen lamp is providing the light.

Figure 4.2 Soft light diffuses the shadows, making them blurry or even fade out gradually. In this case, a white t-shirt was put in front of the halogen bulb to dampen its intensity. (Hey, we're real high-tech at the Carlson world headquarters.)

White balance, indoors

White balance, outdoors

Figure 4.3 Many camcorders feature the capability to adjust the color temperature it displays. It's difficult to tell from these black and white images, but the top picture has a blue cast, while the bottom picture appears a warmer red. (You can see these frames in color at www.peachpit.com/vqs/imovie/)

Color Temperature

White light is a combination of all the colors of the spectrum, as you've seen when playing with a prism or looking at a rainbow. As such, it's not going to always be white while you're filming—a myriad of factors can make images appear with a colored cast, leading to video footage that looks a little too green, or blue, or any number of shifts.

Your camcorder automatically adjusts to compensate for this *color temperature* of the light by setting the white balance. Essentially, this is the color that the camera sees as white, causing the camera to adjust the display of the rest of the colors based on this setting. You probably have a few basic controls for changing the setting, such as Auto, Indoor, or Outdoor presets (**Figure 4.3**).

You may also be able to manually specify the white point by selecting Manual and filming a sheet of white paper in the environment where you'll be shooting; the camera will use the values it captured as the basis for the other colors.

Three-Point Lighting

If you have more control over the way your scene is lit, try to use a basic three-point lighting setup. This allows for plenty of light to illuminate the scene, while also reducing deep shadows. A three-point setup consists of a key light, a fill light, and a back light (**Figure 4.4**).

The key light is the primary light source in your scene, and usually the brightest. The fill light is softer, filling in the shadows and adding texture, and often dimmer than the key light to avoid washing out the image and flattening it. The back light is often small, focused, and used to help separate the scene's subject from the background.

As an easy example, let's say you're setting up to shoot an interview (**Figure 4.5**). Remember this is just a basic configuration—you can position the lights any way you choose.

To set up three-point lighting:

1. With the camera facing the interview subject, position the key light to the right and slightly forward of the camera. Raise the light so that it's at a 35- to 45-degree angle pointing down at the subject.

2. Position the fill light to the left of the camera and subject, approximately half way between the two. The fill prevents deep shadows caused by the key.

3. Place the back light behind the subject, raised a bit higher than the key light, and aimed so that it illuminates the back of the subject's head and shoulders.

Fill light　　*Back light*　　*Key light*

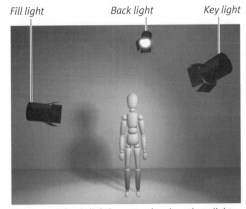

Figure 4.4 A basic lighting setup involves three lights, though of course you can use more (or less).

Key light only

Key light and fill light

 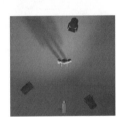

Key, fill, and back lights

Figure 4.5 You could use just a key light, a fill and key, or any other combination of lights. Shown here is the progression of adding lights.

Figure 4.6 A strong light source behind your subjects can easily make them appear as silhouettes.

✔ Tips

- Your camcorder is programmed to automatically adjust the exposure (the amount of light coming in) by opening or closing the iris. You've probably seen this happen when you move from a bright area to a dark one, as details come into view after a second or two. To minimize this extreme change of contrast, break up your shots so that the camera can make the adjustment when you're not filming.

- You've seen the silhouettes. When the key light is behind your subject—whether it's the sun, an especially bright white wall, or a lamp in the background—the camera picks up on the light area in favor of the dark, and pretty soon the person in your video looks like a mob informant protecting his identity (**Figure 4.6**). Try to shoot with the light coming from behind you or from one side so the light is falling on the person or object you're filming.

- When a back light spills directly into the frame, you get the visual artifact known as lens flare. Repositioning your light usually fixes the problem.

- Keep in mind that you don't need to raid a professional camera store and stock up on lighting equipment. You probably have all the lights you need at home or in your office, if you're willing to move things around a bit. Just be careful to not shed too much light onto a scene, which will make it appear flat and less interesting.

- Three-point lighting is a good minimum starting point. On some productions, dozens of light sources may be used to properly light a scene.

Bounce Cards and Reflectors

You don't need a truckload of lights to illuminate your scene. A common and easy solution for shedding more light on your subject is to use a bounce card or reflector (**Figure 4.7**). These are either pieces of cardboard, cloth, or wood colored white, gray, or silver that are used to reflect light into shadowy areas. You can buy inexpensive flexible reflectors that twist into a compact circle for storage. You could also create your own reflectors—white poster board covered with aluminum foil on one side, for example.

Have someone hold the reflector, or mount it on something, and aim its reflection as you would with a fill light.

✔ Tips

■ Bounce light onto a person's face, but don't bounce it into their eyes. Yeah, it's a mean thing to do, but more importantly (for our purposes, anyway), it makes him squint, which hides the eyes, which are often the most compelling part of a person being interviewed.

■ iMovie includes an effect for adjusting the brightness and contrast in a movie clip, but it won't fix a poorly lit scene. In fact, cranking up the brightness too often washes out the image, because the setting is applied evenly throughout the frame. See Chapter 12 to learn how to apply effects in iMovie.

Figure 4.7 A bounce card can be anything that reflects and directs light. In this case, a piece of foam board is being put to good use.

Figure 4.8 Shooting in the middle of the day can create sharp shadows.

Shooting Outside

It's one thing to configure lighting in a dark room where you have absolute control. But the rules become much more slippery when you're filming outside, where the sun and clouds can change the lighting moment-to-moment. No matter where you're filming, you can make choices that take advantage of the weather.

◆ Avoid shooting in the middle of the day when the sun is directly overhead. A key light from above casts shadows down across the face, which obscures a person's eyes and generally gives the appearance of Frankenstein with a hangover (**Figure 4.8**, with apologies to my friends).

◆ Clouds are your friends. A good layer of cloud cover is an excellent diffuser of sunlight, providing a more even level of light in your scene. Coupled with a few well-placed bounce cards and a fill light, a typical cloudy day can provide warmer tones than you might expect.

◆ Shade is also your friend. Again, you want to minimize high-contrast key lighting and enhance the balance between shadows and fill light. Move to the shade of a tree (which can also provide it's own unique shadow textures, depending on the tree) or to the side of a building.

◆ To maximize natural light, shoot early or late in the day, when the sun is near the horizon. The light isn't as harsh, you can get some very intriguing shadows, and the color of the scene is generally warmer and more inviting.

✔ Tip

■ If you must shoot in the middle of a sunny day, put some light-colored fabric above your subject to act as a diffuser.

Capturing Audio

Video gets all the attention. When new camcorders are released, companies hype the image resolution, the color fidelity, the zoom ratios, optics...oh, and there's a microphone in there somewhere, too.

Well, you'll discover soon enough how important audio is. You can spend hours setting up your lighting and composition, but if your sound is poor, your scene is poor. The good news is, for most casual shooters, the built-in mike will capture what you're filming. Some cameras include controls for varying input levels, while most others offer automatic gain control (AGC) to manage the input without your involvement. However, even if you're going to be filming informally, consider purchasing a microphone.

As with lighting, you can spend your life learning the complexities of audio production. This chapter is intended as an overview of some options available for capturing audio.

Headphones

If sound is at all important to you, pack a pair of headphones when you go shooting (**Figure 5.1**). You can use almost any old pair (earbud-style headphones, for example, are extremely portable), but what's important is that you can hear what your camcorder is recording.

When you're standing behind the camera, your ears are naturally picking out the audio in the scene and ignoring other ambient noises. Your camera's microphone isn't nearly as sophisticated, and does its best to maintain a level input based on all the noise in the immediate vicinity. Camcorder mikes can also be sensitive to movement, picking up the sound of you shifting the camera or adjusting the focus.

A pair of headphones screens out the noise around you and gives you a direct bead on what the camera is hearing. And it's the best audio troubleshooting device on the market: if you can't hear your subject, you'll know right away instead of later on when you're editing in iMovie.

Figure 5.1 Wearing headphones while shooting is the only accurate way to know what your camera is recording.

HEADPHONES

Built-in microphone

Figure 5.2 The camera's built-in microphone is good, but it's susceptible to picking up noise from the camera and doesn't record distant objects too well.

Your Camcorder's Microphone

I don't want to give the impression that a camcorder's built-in microphone is a flimsy afterthought. On the contrary, it's a sophisticated device that does the best it can given the circumstances. Where it falls flat at times is its placement: because camcorders are so small, there isn't much room for a microphone (**Figure 5.2**), so you're bound to pick up sounds that the camera is making (such as the motor advancing the tape, or the zoom control adjusting the lens).

Another limitation is distance. The most important factor when recording audio is the distance between the microphone and subject—the closer the better. If you're filming a birthday party, for example, you're likely to be right in the action and will pick up audio pretty well. But what about when you're doing an interview? You want the person's comments to be picked up clearly, but you don't want the camcorder to be in her face. If you're shooting from a moderate distance away (see "Depth of Field" in Chapter 2), the microphone won't pick up the sound clearly.

12-bit versus 16-bit audio

Most likely, your camcorder includes the option to record in 12-bit or 16-bit audio. When you're recording at 12-bit, the microphone is grabbing sound in stereo and saving it to two separate channels (left and right), leaving two more channels to record more audio in the camera later.

If you choose to record in 16-bit audio, the quality is a bit better than CD-quality audio—you're sampling more audio data than in 12-bit mode. (See this book's companion Web site at www.peachpit.com/vqs/imovie for samples of each output.) However, that extra data occupies the available channels, so you can't add more audio to that footage (but see the tip on the next page). More data also means that your footage will take up more disk space in iMovie than 12-bit footage.

Wind Screen mode

Here's a good general tip: read your camcorder manual before you go on vacation. If I hadn't been in such a hurry to take a break, I would have discovered the Wind Screen feature of my camcorder, which does a decent job of cutting down the extra noise produced by wind blowing into the microphone. It's not a perfect solution (what is?), but it would have made some of my footage sound less like I was in the middle of a tornado.

✔ Tips

- Your camcorder can probably let you dub more audio into your footage (for example, if you want to add some narration to a scene), but don't bother. You can do it much better, with less hassle, in iMovie. See Chapter 9 for more on editing audio in iMovie.

- Recording 12-bit audio sounds more flexible, offering two channels free for more sound. However, the advantage is moot because iMovie doesn't recognize separate channels the way other video editing software (like Final Cut Pro) does. So the main benefit you're getting out of using 12-bit is the hard disk savings compared to recording in 16-bit.

- That said, you'd think recording in 16-bit would be the way to go all the time. After all, you want to make sure your audio is the highest quality, right? Well, it depends on how your video is going to turn out. If you're shooting primarily with Quick-Time distribution in mind (see Chapter 14), much of the audio quality is likely to be compressed down to make sure your file sizes aren't insane.

YOUR CAMCORDER'S MICROPHONE

Microphones

Remember earlier how I said you could spend years mastering the art of capturing audio? As with any specialized field, you could also spend a fortune on microphones and audio equipment. The good news is that you can also spend around $20 at Radio Shack and get what you need. Since it's unlikely that you'd spend tens of thousands of dollars on microphones to use with an $800 camcorder, I'm going to stick with a few realistic options.

Lavalier

A simple and portable solution is to purchase a lavalier microphone (**Figure 5.3**). It clips to your shirt or tie, and often has a small battery-powered amplifier, making it a condenser mike, which is how your camcorder's documentation refers to it. (See www.peachpit.com/vqs/imovie for examples of audio captured with and without a lavalier microphone.)

Directional

Directional microphones come in a number of shapes and sizes, and are built to pick up sound in some areas and not others. For example, Cardioid microphones minimize sound coming from the sides and block sound from behind.

A shotgun mike, like the one found on higher-end camcorders (**Figure 5.4**), picks up audio only in front of the camera (or whatever the mike is pointed at) while ignoring sound from behind the mike (therefore reducing the likelihood of recording camera noise).

An omnidirectional microphone, on the other hand, picks up sound from all sides and is good to use when you're not focused on any one particular subject.

Figure 5.3 A simple clip-on lavalier microphone can greatly increase the quality of your recorded audio.

Directional microphone

Figure 5.4 Higher-end digital camcorders are outfitted with directional microphones that aren't as likely to pick up camera (or camera operator) noise.

Wireless

Wireless microphones also come in a variety of shapes and sizes, but aren't tied to an audio cable that snakes back to the camcorder. They're portable, allowing you more freedom to shoot your video while moving, or from anywhere in the room. The biggest drawback to using a wireless mike is that it's more likely to pick up interference from other radio sources, so be sure to test the output before you start filming and use headphones to monitor the recording while shooting.

✔ Tips

■ Check your camcorder's specifications for attaching external microphones. Some require that the mike is amplified, calling for an external power source. Other cameras can use the camcorder's battery to provide power.

■ If you don't entirely trust your camcorder's mike, or just want to be sure you have a backup source of audio, consider purchasing a MiniDisc recorder. It stores audio digitally, which you can import into iMovie and add to your movie, or use in place of audio that didn't record clearly (due to the placement of the microphone, for example). If you're dubbing dialogue, you may have to break the audio into several clips in iMovie and synchronize the timing often, but that's a better solution than trying to recreate the original shoot. See Chapter 9 for more on editing audio.

Ambient Sound

Your biggest concern is likely to be capturing the audio of your main subject, but don't forget about ambient noise. The sounds that surround you can be just as important as the main audio to establish mood or place. It's also good for maintaining *consistent* noise. For example, I took some footage on the plane en route to my aforementioned vacation, but when I brought it into iMovie, the engine noise differed depending on when the video was shot (when we started to descend) and even what side of the plane I was taping. However, I was able to use a sample of ambient noise in the background to provide an even level of noise (and also to adjust the audio so it wasn't as dominant). Record ambient noise whenever you can—you can spend a few minutes before or after your primary shooting and get plenty of material to work with later in iMovie.

MICROPHONES

Part 2
Editing

iMovie Overview

Being a fan of the moviemaking process, I enjoy reading "behind the scenes" articles about how films are produced. In nearly all cases, the reporter interviews cast and crew at the movie set during shooting (and invariably makes it sound more exciting than it usually is). But filming is only one part of the production.

Rarely reported is the editing stage, when the editor and director spend long hours in a dark editing room—sometimes for many months—shaping hours of raw footage into what we eventually see in a theater. They grab the best takes from each day's shooting, assemble them according to the storyline, and then add transitions, audio, special effects, and whatever else is required for that particular flick.

The process of making a digital video is the same (minus the reporters). By this point you've shot your footage, but that doesn't mean you have a movie. Here's where iMovie and digital non-linear editing can take your mass of video and audio and turn it into a movie. This chapter introduces iMovie, making sure you have the tools you need to get started, and giving you an overview tour of the program's unexpectedly powerful yet simple interface.

Getting iMovie

If you've purchased a new FireWire-equipped Macintosh in the last year or so, you should have a free copy of iMovie 2 on your hard disk or on an accompanying CD-ROM.

If your Mac is slightly older, or didn't include a FireWire port (such as some iMacs, Power-Books, and early iBooks), you can purchase iMovie for $50 through Apple's online store (http://store.apple.com/).

However, if you're running Mac OS X but don't have iMovie, you're in luck. To encourage people to upgrade to its next-generation operating system, Apple currently (as of Fall 2001) includes iMovie 2 for Mac OS X with Mac OS X 10.1.

Figure 6.1 Launching iMovie the first time gives you a short title movie and buttons for getting started.

Figure 6.2 iMovie comes with no manual—instead, you can follow along with the online tutorial.

Working with Projects

The first thing to do is launch iMovie. This step may seem absurdly obvious, but stick with me for a minute. Launch the application by double-clicking its icon within the Finder. After the program's interface appears, a dialog box offers the following options (**Figure 6.1**):

◆ **New Project** creates an iMovie project from scratch. After clicking the button, give your project a name and location.

◆ **Open Project** loads an existing project. In the window that appears, locate the project file on your hard disk.

◆ **Open Tutorial** loads the iMovie tutorial files stored on your hard disk. To then run the step-by-step tutorial, select iMovie Tutorial from the Help menu (**Figure 6.2**). If you downloaded the program (which doesn't include the tutorial files), or if you've deleted the files, this button does not appear.

◆ **Quit** exits the program. (When this dialog box is displayed, the Quit command under the File menu is disabled.)

Folder Structure under Mac OS X

Mac OS X doesn't store the iMovie application in a folder as in Mac OS 9. Instead, it's a package, containing the program and associated files. If you're installing new plug-ins, for example, there's no Plug-ins folder to put them in. Instead, you'd need to go to the Users folder on your hard disk, open the folder with your user name, then open the Library folder. Create a new folder called iMovie, and within that folder create one called Plug-ins. This isn't required to use iMovie, but it's good to know for the future.

Figure 6.3 An iMovie project is made up of a small project file (top) and a Media folder containing raw video and audio files.

Replacing the Title Movie

The video in the initial dialog box is fun to watch...once or twice. Personalize iMovie under Mac OS 9 by using your own splash movie (this doesn't work in Mac OS X).

To replace the title movie:

1. Take a video clip you've created with iMovie or other software (such as QuickTime Pro), and export it as a QuickTime movie measuring 320 by 240 pixels. (I'm jumping ahead a little here; we'll cover exporting later.)

2. In the Finder, rename the clip "SplashSmall.mov".

3. Open the Resources folder located within the iMovie application folder.

4. Move or rename the existing SplashSmall.mov file, and replace it with the file you created.

The next time you launch iMovie, your movie will be used as the title movie. You can also create a video measuring 640 by 480 pixels to replace the file Splash.mov, which comes up when you select About iMovie from the Apple menu.

Opening and closing projects

Most programs, such as Microsoft Word or Adobe Photoshop, work with individual files you can create, open, and save. iMovie works just a tad differently.

An iMovie project comprises a project file and its associated media files. The project file is miniscule in comparison to the others: the iMovie tutorial, for example, includes an 8K project file called "iMovie Tutorial," and a folder called "Media" that's 160 MB (**Figure 6.3**). The project file is small because it only records how you've arranged and edited the media files (I'll go into more detail about this in Chapter 8).

When you begin working within iMovie, you'll soon notice something different from other programs: *there is no Close command.* Once you've created or opened a project file, the only way to close it is by creating or opening a different project, or by quitting the program.

On the other hand, iMovie remembers which project you're working on between sessions, so your current project automatically loads the next time you launch the program, thereby skipping the initial dialog box.

✔ Tips

- iMovie looks at your Mac's File Sharing control panel settings to display the owner name when saving a file, which is why you see "Jeff Carlson's Movie" instead of something like "Untitled". Your computer hasn't suddenly become sentient.

- When you're finished running through the tutorial, you can delete the iMovie Tutorial folder to regain 160 MB of disk space. Besides, with this book in hand, who needs an online tutorial?

iMovie's Interface

iMovie's interface is probably different from most programs you're used to. It occupies the entire screen, whether you want it to or not (**Figure 6.4**), even including a backdrop pattern that obscures the Finder. And iMovie isn't shy about monopolizing the space: foreground items such as Mac OS 9's Control Strip and Mac OS X's Dock are hidden when iMovie is the front-most application.

The interface comprises three main areas: the Monitor, where you view video clips; the Shelf, where clips are stored; and the combined Clip Viewer and Timeline Viewer, where you assemble your movie.

Clip Viewer   Timeline Viewer   Monitor   Shelf

Figure 6.4 iMovie occupies the entire screen, and is broken down into three main sections: the Monitor, the Shelf, and the combined Clip Viewer and Timeline Viewer.

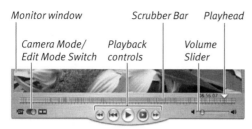

Monitor window   Scrubber Bar   Playhead

Camera Mode/   Playback   Volume
Edit Mode Switch   controls   Slider

Figure 6.5 iMovie groups its Monitor controls in a relatively small space.

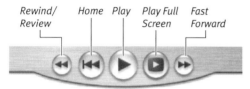

Rewind/   Home   Play   Play Full   Fast
Review   Screen   Forward

Figure 6.6 Use these Monitor controls when you're in iMovie's Edit Mode. Don't you wish your VCR had these groovy liquid/glass buttons?

The Monitor

The Monitor is where you view and edit clips. A few controls, such as the Scrubber Bar, affect how you edit your clips (**Figure 6.5**). The playback controls are context-sensitive, and can play clips (**Figure 6.6**) or control a camcorder (**Figure 6.7**, next page).

Monitor controls

◆ **Monitor window.** View clips and incoming video from a camcorder.

◆ **Camera Mode/Edit Mode Switch.** Toggle between these modes to either import or edit video footage.

◆ **Volume Slider.** Set the playback volume by dragging the knob or clicking a spot on the slider.

◆ **Playhead.** Drag the Playhead to any point within your movie or clip; the numbers beside it indicate the time location within the movie.

◆ **Scrubber Bar.** When viewing an entire movie, the Scrubber Bar includes lines marking clips and transitions. This is also where you can select portions of clips and cut, copy, or crop them (see Chapter 8).

Playback controls (Edit Mode)

◆ **Rewind/Review.** Click this button to play the video backwards quickly; click it again to stop playback.

◆ **Home.** Click here to move to the start of the movie (or clip, if selected in the Shelf).

◆ **Play.** Click this button to play the video in real time. Click it again to stop playback.

◆ **Play Full Screen.** This button expands the video to fill the entire screen.

◆ **Fast Forward.** Click to play the video forward quickly; click again to stop.

Playback controls (Camera Mode)

◆ **Import.** With a camera attached, click this button to begin saving the video to your hard disk. Click it again to stop capturing.

◆ **Rewind/Review.** Click this button to rewind the camcorder's tape. If the tape is playing, click and hold to review (play backwards) the footage quickly. Releasing the button resumes normal playback.

◆ **Pause.** Click this button to pause, but still view, the camera's playback.

◆ **Play.** Click this button to play the video in real time.

◆ **Stop.** This button stops the camcorder's tape.

◆ **Fast Forward.** Click to advance the tape without playing it. As with the Rewind/Review control, if the tape is playing, click and hold to view the playback quickly. Releasing the button resumes normal playback.

✔ Tips

■ When switching between Camera Mode and Edit Mode, simply click the icons—you don't have to "move" the switch.

■ In Edit Mode, the spacebar activates and deactivates the Play button. In Camera Mode, the spacebar activates the Import button.

■ Use the up and down arrow keys on your keyboard to increase or decrease the playback volume.

■ Use the left and right arrow keys to move the video in one-frame increments when you're in Edit Mode. Hold Shift and use the arrow keys to move 10 frames at a time.

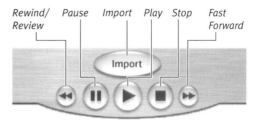

Figure 6.7 With Camera Mode enabled, the buttons control the camera's playback functions.

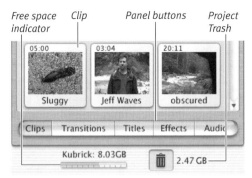

Free space indicator *Clip* *Panel buttons* *Project Trash*

Figure 6.8 The Shelf, in addition to storing clips, displays free hard disk space, the size of the Trash, and serves as the panel for controlling other features such as transitions and titles.

The Shelf

Think of the Shelf as a big rack filled with numerous videocassettes (but much better organized); this is where you store your raw footage in preparation for editing (**Figure 6.8**). It's also where you find controls for working with transitions, titles, effects, and audio options.

Shelf components

◆ **Clips.** The purpose of the Shelf is to store your clips, which are arranged in a grid. Use the scroll bar at right to view more clips.

◆ **Panel buttons.** The Shelf doubles as the control center for the Transitions, Titles, Effects, and Audio panels. (Technically, I guess it should be called the Shelf panel, but that's like saying I drive an automobile vehicle.) Click one of the buttons to activate its panel.

◆ **Free space indicator.** The bar fills from left to right according to the amount of available space on the hard disk where your project is stored, which is listed above. A green bar indicates plenty of free space; yellow warns you that you're getting low; and red means you're critically low on space.

◆ **Project Trash.** When you delete clips, they're sent to the Project Trash. However, this trash doesn't operate the same as the Trash in the Finder: you can't open it and pull things out. The reason for this is a bit convoluted and explained in Chapter 7. For now, just be aware that the size of the Project Trash is indicated to the right of the icon.

iMovie's Interface

Clip Viewer and Timeline Viewer

The Shelf may hold all of your raw video clips, but you don't have a movie until you start moving them to the Clip Viewer or Timeline Viewer. Consider them to be two different methods of looking at the structure of your movie. The Clip Viewer displays clips in the order that they play, with large thumbnail previews to help identify them (**Figure 6.9**). The Timeline Viewer arranges the clips in order and also depicts their lengths (**Figures 6.11**, **6.12**, and **6.13**). The Timeline also includes audio tracks and controls for changing aspects of a clip, which I'll discuss in the next few chapters.

Clip Viewer components

◆ **Clip Viewer tab.** Click the eye icon to bring the Clip Viewer to the front.

◆ **Project title** and **movie length.** Located at the top-left corner of the Clip Viewer, these labels tell you which project is open, and the total length of the movie. The type of movie, either NTSC or PAL, is shown in parentheses.

◆ **Transitions.** When you add a transition to your movie, an icon indicates which clip it's attached to (see Chapter 10).

Clip Viewer tab   Project title   Movie length   Transition   Clip

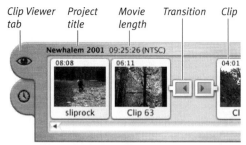

Figure 6.9 Using the Clip Viewer is often easier than the Timeline Viewer when adding clips.

Figure 6.10 The Views tab in iMovie's preferences includes options for changing how clips are shown.

Changing View Preferences

You can tweak some of the ways clips are displayed by setting options in the Views tab of iMovie's preferences (**Figure 6.10**).

◆ **Show Thumbnails in Timeline.** When enabled, a small preview of the clip's first frame appears in the Timeline Viewer.

◆ **Use Short Time Codes.** This option truncates time codes; a 10-second clip appears as "10:00" instead of "00:10:00".

◆ **Show More Details.** Turning this off removes the clip name and time code from clips in the Timeline Viewer.

◆ **Show Locked Audio Only When Selected.** You can lock audio clips individually, which are shown with a pin icon (see Chapter 9). This shows the icon only when the clip is selected.

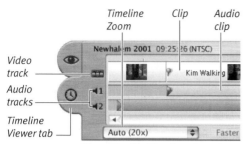

Figure 6.11 The Timeline gives you a better sense of how much time each clip occupies.

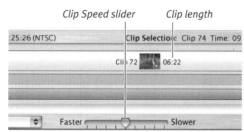

Figure 6.12 Speed up or apply slow-motion to a clip using the Clip Speed slider.

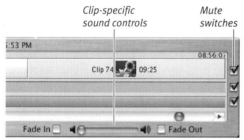

Figure 6.13 The sound controls at the bottom apply to selected clips, while the Mute switches turn track audio on and off.

Timeline Viewer components

◆ **Timeline Viewer tab.** Click the clock icon to bring this viewer to the front.

◆ **Video track.** The first horizontal bar with the filmstrip icon represents the video track, where clips are displayed according to their lengths. Transitions also appear here, with an icon similar to those found in the Clip Viewer.

◆ **Audio tracks.** iMovie gives you two separate audio tracks to work with, indicated by the speaker icons. Audio can be extracted from video clips or imported and edited on these tracks.

◆ **Timeline Zoom popup menu.** This control determines how much of the timeline is shown in the viewer: 1x shows the entire movie, while 50x may display only a few seconds, depending on your movie's length. Zooming in is often helpful when you're editing small clips or transitions.

◆ **Clip Speed slider.** When a clip is selected, use this slider to control how fast or slow the clip plays.

◆ **Clip-specific sound controls.** The volume slider and Fade In/Fade Out checkboxes apply only to a selected clip (see Chapter 9).

◆ **Mute switches.** Uncheck a box to turn off the volume in its associated video or audio track. This doesn't affect any volume adjustments you've made to particular clips (see Chapter 9).

iMOVIE'S INTERFACE

Monitoring Your Movies

iMovie's Monitor window is invaluable, and the Play Full Screen feature is helpful when you need to get a better feel for how the movie will display. However, consider hooking up an external television or AV monitor so you can see how your movie will really look to your audience (**Figure 6.14**). (If your movies are destined only for display on the Web or via email, you may not want to go to this trouble.)

You'll need your computer, a television or monitor with RCA-style input jacks, and your digital camcorder. You'll also need the FireWire cable used to hook up your camera, and the AV cable that came with the camcorder that allows you to view movies on a TV (it normally has three connectors on one end—yellow, red, and white—and a single connector that plugs into the camera).

To hook up an external video monitor:

1. Connect the camera to your computer via the FireWire cable.

2. Connect the television to your camera using the AV cable.

3. Switch the television's mode from TV to Video, if necessary.

4. In iMovie, choose Preferences from the Edit menu (or the iMovie menu in Mac OS X).

5. Switch to the Advanced tab, and click the Video Play Through to Camera checkbox.

6. Click OK to exit the Preferences dialog box. Your movie should now appear on the TV.

✔ Tip

■ Plug in the camera's AC adapter while you're working, so you're not draining your battery while at your desk.

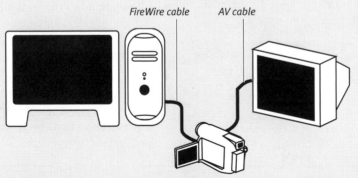

FireWire cable   *AV cable*

Figure 6.14 Adding an external television or monitor to your iMovie setup lets you see how the video appears on a real video screen.

IMPORTING FOOTAGE

When I first began looking into buying a camcorder, cost was definitely a main consideration. I found several analog cameras in the $200 to $300 range, which was acceptable. However, all signs point to a digital future—but the cameras cost around $700 or (in some cases much) higher. Sure, digital is definitely the future, but did I really need to edge into that higher price range? I wanted the camera primarily for vacations and special events, so the quality and features of a digital camcorder probably weren't worth the extra money…right?

Wrong.

If you're planning on doing any type of video editing (and I'm assuming you are, since you're reading this book), spend the extra bucks and go digital. I can't stress this point enough. The convenience of hooking your camera directly to your Mac and just letting the video flow is worth the money you put out up-front. You also get the benefit of clearer video and audio, since the footage is entirely digital and therefore doesn't need to undergo any analog to digital conversion.

However, don't let my digital zeal frighten you. If you already own an analog camcorder, you can still use iMovie to edit it, as I'll discuss later in this chapter.

Importing Clips

Getting footage into iMovie is a snap: connect your digital camcorder to your Mac via FireWire, and start importing. You don't even need to shut down your Mac to plug in the FireWire cable (as we needed to do in the days of SCSI devices). Your only practical limitation is space on your hard drive—make sure you have plenty (see the sidebar on the next page).

To connect via FireWire:

1. Quit iMovie if it's running. Apple recommends quitting iMovie before you plug or unplug FireWire cables.

2. Plug the FireWire cable into the Mac and the camcorder.

3. Switch the camcorder to VCR or Play mode.

4. Launch iMovie. If you don't have a project file yet, create a new one and name it. The Monitor switches to Camera mode and displays "Camera Connected" along with the time marker of the tape (**Figure 7.1**).

To import footage from the camcorder:

1. Use the Monitor's Playback controls to rewind or forward the camcorder's tape to the spot where you want to begin.

2. Click the Import button. The imported footage is stored as clips in the Shelf (**Figure 7.2**).

3. Click the Import button again to stop.

Figure 7.1 Connecting the camera to your Mac via FireWire automatically switches iMovie to Camera mode.

Figure 7.2 iMovie can automatically detect when scenes begin and end, and split them into clips.

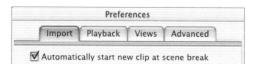

Figure 7.3 Turning off the Automatically start new clip at scene break option reduces the number of clips created from your footage when you import.

By default, iMovie creates a new clip for each scene, which is calculated based on the time stamps stored on the tape. If you prefer, the video can be stored in fewer clips, giving you the option to *manually* control where clips are split. (iMovie limits the clip size to 2 GB, which is about 9 minutes of video, so you can't just import all your footage as one gigantic clip.) However, I've found that leaving iMovie's automatic scene detection on saves time later when I'm editing.

To turn off automatic scene detection:

1. Open iMovie's preferences.

2. On the Import tab, deselect the option labeled Automatically start new clip at scene break (**Figure 7.3**). Click OK.

✔ Tips

- Are are you you hearing hearing double double? There's a slight lag between the camera and the Mac when importing; turn the volume all the way down on either the camcorder or in iMovie.

- If you want to import your video to an external FireWire hard drive, make sure the drive has a speed of at least 7,200 RPM. Although some users report that 5,400 RPM drives work fine, a faster drive is less likely to drop frames or audio when importing.

The Biggest Hard Drive Isn't Large Enough

When you begin working with digital video, your concept of hard disk space changes forever. For example, one second of footage equals 3.6 MB on disk.

Fortunately, hard drives are getting cheaper: a quick search for a 60 GB drive turns up prices between $150 and $200 as of this writing (try www.dealmac.com). Here's one way to estimate how much storage you need, courtesy of Jay Nelson's *Design Tools Monthly* newsletter (www.design-tools.com):

To determine a disk's DV capacity:

1. Divide the disk capacity by 3.6 MB, which is the amount of space required to save one second of digital video.

2. Divide that result by 60 to convert from seconds to minutes.

For example, a 60 GB hard disk can hold 277.77 minutes of digital video (60,000 MB / 3.6 MB = 16,666.67 seconds / 60 = 2,777.77 minutes).

In addition to importing video from the camcorder's tape, you can grab live footage directly from the camera.

To import live footage from the camcorder:

1. With the camera connected to your Mac, launch iMovie.

2. Switch the camcorder to Camera or Record mode.

3. In iMovie's preferences, click the Advanced tab (**Figure 7.4**).

4. Click the Video Play Through to Camera option, then click OK.

5. Switch iMovie to Camera mode and click the Import button. You don't need to use the camera's Record button.

6. Click the Import button again to stop.

As clips are imported, they're stored in order on the Shelf with the expectation that you're going to crop and rearrange them when they're put into the movie. But suppose you're importing footage that's already been edited, or is otherwise in the correct order? You can save a few steps by importing the clips directly to the Clip Viewer.

To import to the Clip Viewer instead of the Shelf:

1. Open iMovie's preferences, which displays the Import tab (**Figure 7.5**).

2. In the Imported Clips Go To box, click the Movie radio button. Click OK.

3. Click the Import button to begin capturing the footage, then click Import again to stop.

Figure 7.4 The Video Play Through to Camera option enables you to import video as you record it.

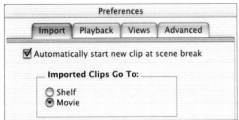

Figure 7.5 Set the Imported Clips Go To preference to Movie to import footage directly to the Clip Viewer.

IMPORTING CLIPS

Figure 7.6 Analog-to-video converters enable you to use a non-digital camcorder with iMovie.

Importing Footage from an Analog Camcorder

The process of importing footage from an analog camcorder in iMovie is much the same as when importing from a digital camcorder. However, you need a go-between device that converts the camcorder's analog signal to digital information on the Mac. Products such as Dazzle's $300 Hollywood DV-Bridge (`www.dazzle.com`) feature a FireWire port for connecting to your computer and RCA-style inputs for connecting to your camcorder; some devices may also include an S-Video port (**Figure 7.6**).

Since you're importing converted analog data, iMovie doesn't automatically split clips according to scenes. You'll have to use iMovie's editing tools to trim and organize the clips, or manually start and stop importing according to scenes.

To import from a non-DV camcorder:

1. Connect the conversion device to the Mac via FireWire, and to the camera using RCA or S-Video cabling.

2. Switch the camcorder to VCR or Play mode.

3. Push the camcorder's Play button.

4. Click the Import button in iMovie.

5. When finished, click Import again to stop capturing video, and press the Stop button on the camcorder.

Importing Old VHS Tapes Using a DV Camcorder

If you have a digital camcorder, but still have some older VHS (or other format) tapes, you can bring that footage into iMovie to edit or even just store digitally. Connect your VCR to your camcorder and record the contents of the VHS tape to the DV tape. Then you can import your footage into iMovie normally.

Another option is to use a recent Sony DV camcorder, which performs the analog-to-digital conversion.

Analog tape doesn't last forever—save your wedding/graduation/school play on disk (and maybe even edit out a few of those more embarrassing moments).

Importing Still Pictures

The images in your movie don't have to all fly by at 30 frames per second. iMovie can easily import photos you've scanned or taken with a digital still camera—or better yet, images that you've modified in an image-editing program such as Adobe Photoshop (www.adobe.com/products/photoshop/) or GraphicConverter (www.lemkesoft.com). When you import a still image, it becomes a movie clip with a length of 5 seconds. But first, make sure it's ready to be imported into iMovie.

To prepare a still picture for import:

1. Open the image in your favorite image-editing application.

2. Crop the image so that its dimensions are 640 by 480 pixels (**Figure 7.7**). Make any changes you see fit.

3. Save the image as a JPEG or PICT file.

To import a still picture:

1. In iMovie, choose Import File from the File menu (or press Command-I).

2. In the Import File dialog box, select the still image you want (**Figure 7.8**) and click the Import button. The image appears as a clip on the Shelf, which can be added to your movie like any other clip (**Figure 7.9**).

✔ Tip

■ Imported images that don't measure 640 by 480 pixels are resized by iMovie to accommodate their size, resulting in black bands appearing on the sides or top and bottom, depending on the orientation of the image.

Figure 7.7 To fit correctly into a movie, still images must measure 640 by 480 pixels.

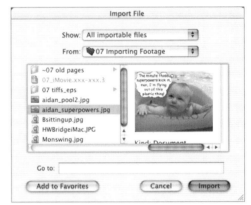

Figure 7.8 iMovie can import images formatted as JPEG or PICT files (iMovie for Mac OS X shown here).

Figure 7.9 Come on, did you honestly think I could write an iMovie book and not include a baby picture?

Figure 7.10 To import QuickTime movies into iMovie, you must first convert them in QuickTime Player.

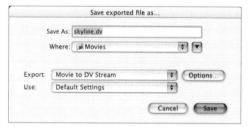

Figure 7.11 The Pro version of QuickTime Player can export movies to the DV format.

Figure 7.12 The imported DV clip ("skyline.dv") appears on the Shelf with the other clips.

Importing QuickTime Movies

The first time I launched iMovie, I was baffled. Surely, a program that uses QuickTime so heavily would be able to import the Quick-Time format, right? Apparently not. iMovie can only import DV media. However, you *can* import DV footage that was once a QuickTime movie, using the Pro version of QuickTime Player.

To convert a QuickTime movie to DV:

1. Open the QuickTime movie in QuickTime Player (**Figure 7.10**).

2. Choose Export from the File menu.

3. In the dialog box that appears, specify where you want to save the converted file and choose Movie to DV Stream from the Export pop-up menu (**Figure 7.11**). The file's extension will automatically be changed to ".dv".

4. Click the Save button.

To import the converted movie into iMovie:

1. In iMovie, choose Import File from the File menu.

2. Locate the file in the Import File dialog box, then click the Import button. The clip appears on the Shelf (**Figure 7.12**).

✔ Tips

- Most QuickTime movies are small in size and compressed, which is great for viewing on the Web but not so good looking compared to a DV clip taken from a video camcorder. So don't be surprised if the clip looks highly pixelated or blocky.

- You can import media files from other iMovie projects, which are also in the DV format.

How iMovie Manages Clips

If you're casually flipping through this chapter, I'll understand it if you skip everything else—*except this section*. It's important to understand how iMovie handles clips as you're working with them, especially when you begin deleting unused clips.

Clips can be made up of either video footage or imported still pictures. Each clip includes a thumbnail image of the clip's first frame, a time code noting the clip's duration, and a title (**Figure 7.13**).

When you import footage, iMovie creates a new clip for each scene, which then adds a new clip file to your hard disk. However, even if you rename, split, reverse, or otherwise edit a clip in iMovie, *the media file stays the same* (**Figure 7.14**). iMovie actually records only the changes made to the clip, and doesn't change the clip's original media file.

This clip management style comes in handy in several ways as you use iMovie.

Advantages of iMovie's method of managing clips

◆ **Undo.** iMovie offers 10 levels of Undo, enabling you to recombine split clips, move clips back to their original locations, and other actions.

◆ **Deleting clips.** iMovie's Trash is something of a digital Roach Motel: clips go in, but they don't come out! This doesn't mean the clips are gone for good, though (see "Moving Clips to the Trash," later in this chapter).

◆ **Restoring clips.** If you're not happy with your edits, or something has gone horribly wrong, you can always restore the clip to its original state, because the original data is always on file. See the next chapter to learn how to restore clips.

Figure 7.13 Each clip contains a thumbnail image of the first frame in the video. If a clip has been split, iMovie adds a number to indicate it's a section from the original.

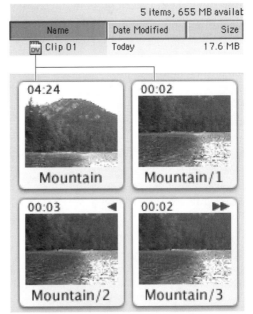

Figure 7.14 The original clip was renamed "Mountain" and split into four separate clips, but the clip's original data file remains intact.

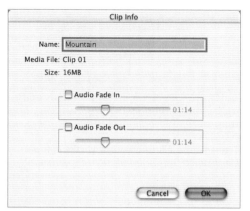

Figure 7.15 Double-clicking a clip displays the Clip Info dialog box, which shows the media file's name.

Figure 7.16 Click and drag your pointer in the Shelf's background area to select multiple clips (highlighted in yellow, though it's hard to tell here).

Managing Clips

Clips are named sequentially during import (such as "Clip 01"), but you can rename them with more meaningful titles. If you split a clip (explained in the next chapter), iMovie adds a slash and a number to indicate it's part of the original, such as "Mountain/1".

To rename a clip:

1. Click the clip's title, which selects the text. Or, either double-click the clip or press Command-Shift-I to display the Clip Info dialog box (**Figure 7.15**).

2. Type a new name and hit Return, or click OK in the Clip Info dialog box.

The Shelf features slots for storing clips, but it doesn't matter in what order they appear. You'll find yourself moving them frequently as you assemble your movie.

To reorder clips in the Shelf:

1. Click the clip(s) you wish to move. To grab a range of clips, click and drag a box around them with the pointer, or Shift-click multiple clips. Selected clips appear highlighted in yellow (**Figure 7.16**).

2. Click and drag the clip(s) to a new location in the Shelf.

✔ Tips

■ Renaming a clip only changes its name in iMovie. The original media file is still named "Clip 04" (or similar). Do not rename the media file on disk or iMovie will lose track of it.

■ Since you can drag clips anywhere in the Shelf, use this capability to visually group scenes or related materials before you add them to your movie.

MANAGING CLIPS

Moving Clips to the Trash

One of the few elements of iMovie that vexes me is the Trash, which seems at first straight-forward, but doesn't act the way you would expect. You can easily delete clips, which are sent to the Trash, but there's no way to open the Trash and pull a deleted clip out (a behavior that every Mac user is accustomed to in the Finder).

To delete a clip:

1. Select a clip.

2. Press the Delete key, or click and drag the clip to the Trash icon (**Figure 7.17**).

So far, so simple. Remember that iMovie isn't actually deleting any file from your hard disk, only keeping track of which portions of clips have been sent to the Trash (**Figure 7.18**).

Emptying the Trash

If you know you're not going to need any of the deleted clips later, you can empty the Trash. This action permanently deletes the media files (or portions of the files, depend-ing on what was cut), and frees up the amount of disk space indicated next to the Trash icon.

However, emptying the Trash also perma-nently affects most of your clips—you can't use the Undo command, or restore clips to their original state. So unless you desperately need to reclaim some hard disk space, *don't empty the Trash until your movie is finished.*

To empty the Trash:

1. Choose Empty Trash from the File menu.

2. iMovie displays a warning (**Figure 7.19**). Click OK to empty the Trash, or click Cancel to leave its contents untouched.

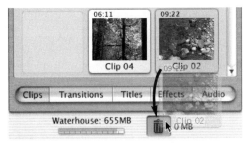

Figure 7.17 To delete a clip, drag it to the Trash, or simply select the clip and press the Delete key.

Figure 7.18 As clips are added, the Trash indicates how much footage is marked for deletion.

Figure 7.19 I usually think reminder dialog boxes are annoying, but this is one I always pay attention to.

MOVING CLIPS TO THE TRASH

Figure 7.20 Resurrect your trashed footage by quitting iMovie without saving changes.

✔ Tips

- Levels of Undo don't transfer between your editing sessions. When you quit iMovie then launch it again later, your last 10 actions are forgotten.

- One way to restore clips you've trashed is to quit iMovie without saving changes to your project (**Figure 7.20**). When you launch it again, the clips you threw away will be intact again (though you lose all other edits you made since the last save).

- Don't forget that even if you empty the Trash, you still have a backup of your clips: the original footage stored on your camcorder's tape.

- Sometimes it can take a while to empty the Trash, due to the way iMovie stores the clip media files. Deleting a short section at the beginning of a clip, for example, makes emptying the Trash take longer because iMovie must first copy the clip's remaining data, calculate the time between the new beginning and the ending, then delete the original file. Trashing a section from the end of a clip is quicker, because iMovie already knows the clip's beginning point.

MOVING CLIPS TO THE TRASH

Transferring Clips to Other Projects

As you'll learn in the next chapter, non-linear editing means you don't have to stick to the chronology of the camcorder's tape. What if you want to insert your great bear sighting that you took days earlier? Moving clips is easy, though a little rough around the edges.

To transfer a clip to another project:

1. Open the project that contains the clip you want.

2. Identify the clip's media file by double-clicking the clip and noting its name.

3. Switch from iMovie to the Finder and locate that media file in your project's Media folder.

4. Move the file to your destination project's Media folder (**Figure 7.21**).

5. Open the destination project. A dialog box tells you that iMovie has found clips that weren't originally there (**Figure 7.22**). Click OK.

6. Save your project, then open the other project where the clip originated. iMovie displays a dialog box telling you that the clip's media file could not be found and was skipped (**Figure 7.23**). Click OK.

7. Open the destination project again, where the clip now appears on the Shelf.

✔ Tips

- Unfortunately, if you've moved several clips, you must confirm a dialog box in the original project for each missing media file.

- Use this technique to split larger project folders into smaller ones when copying to smaller-capacity hard disks.

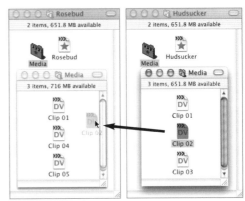

Figure 7.21 Perform a little quick-change act to move clips between projects—iMovie figures it out.

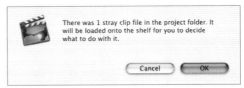

Figure 7.22 iMovie notices the new media file and builds a thumbnail for the clip.

Figure 7.23 When you open a project, iMovie scans the Media folder to see if there have been any changes. When a file goes missing, you get this message.

EDITING VIDEO

The first movies were pure documentaries. Armed with new technology, camera operators shot what they saw: trains leaving the station, people at work, the movement of animals. Motion pictures didn't need to tell a story because the story was in the reproduction. The first movie created by brothers Louis and Auguste Lumière was the action spectacular *Workers Leaving the Lumière Factory*, depicting exactly that.

However, filmmakers soon realized that their "flickers" didn't need to be just linear slices of life. They could shoot movies in any order and assemble them to tell a story, or even combine totally unrelated scenes for dramatic effect. Lev Kuleshov, an early Russian filmmaker, filmed a closeup of an actor wearing a neutral expression. He then intercut a scene of an empty bowl, prompting audiences to praise the actor's subtle portrayal of hunger. Kuleshov took the same neutral footage and intercut scenes of a dead woman in a coffin, then a girl playing with a doll, and in each case audiences were amazed to see the actor's grief or joy. Editing became a vehicle for expressing emotions or ideas that weren't necessarily present during filming.

Today, iMovie and non-linear editing give you the capability to use the visual language of film to tell stories, whether fiction or simply a day at the park. The fun begins here.

Time Code

In Chapter 2, I explained how time code works as it applies to a camcorder. Although it operates the same in iMovie (00:00:00:00 represents hours:minutes:seconds:frames), you're going to run into it in different places while editing.

Time code in iMovie

◆ **At the Playhead.** The Playhead's time code always shows the time relative to the entire movie. So, for example, positioning the Playhead two seconds into a clip that appears in the middle of your movie displays something like "15:14" instead of "02:00" (**Figure 8.1**). The only exception is when you select a clip on the Shelf, which isn't yet part of your movie.

◆ **In the Clip Viewer.** In addition to showing time code of individual clips, the Clip Viewer and Timeline Viewer display the movie's total length. The Thumbnail Playhead, a red inverted T, indicates where the Playhead appears (**Figure 8.2**).

◆ **In the Timeline Viewer.** Although the Playhead in the scrubber bar shows a time code, you often need to refer to the Timeline Viewer (and its Playhead) when editing. Individual clips include a time code indicating their length, as space permits (**Figure 8.3**).

Playhead time code

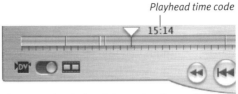

Figure 8.1 The Playhead time code refers to time location within the context of the movie, even if only a single clip is selected.

Total movie length   *Thumbnail Playhead*

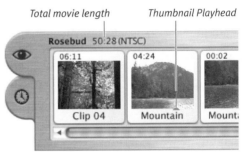

Figure 8.2 A Thumbnail Playhead appears in the Clip Viewer, but without a time code.

Playhead location time code   *Clip length*

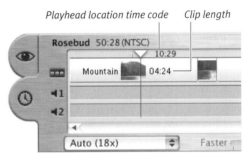

Figure 8.3 The Playhead in the Timeline Viewer includes its own time code, which is based on the movie's total time.

Figure 8.4 Drag clips from the Shelf to the Clip Viewer (shown) or Timeline Viewer to add them to the movie.

Highlighted bar

Figure 8.5 In the Timeline Viewer, a bright blue vertical bar indicates where a clip will be inserted.

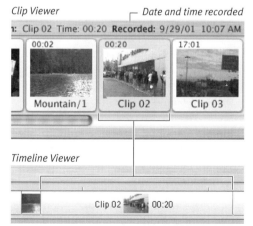

Clip Viewer   *Date and time recorded*

Timeline Viewer

Figure 8.6 The two views shown here are of the same clip. The Timeline Viewer displays an approximation of the clip's length.

Adding Clips to the Movie

Even with a bunch of clips on the Shelf, your movie doesn't exist until you begin building it in the Clip Viewer or the Timeline Viewer.

To add clips to the movie:

1. Select one or more clips in the Shelf.

2. Drag the clip(s) to the Clip Viewer or the Timeline Viewer (**Figure 8.4**).

Ordering Clips

The movie's order progresses from left to right in the Viewers, so use the Clip Viewer to drag and drop clips in the order you wish them to appear; iMovie politely moves existing clips aside in the Clip Viewer to indicate where you can drop your clip. When dragging clips from the Shelf to the Timeline Viewer, a highlighted bar helps you see where clips begin and end—especially useful when you have many short clips (**Figure 8.5**).

✔ Tips

- It's easier to assemble your movie by dragging clips to the Clip Viewer where each clip icon is the same size. The Timeline Viewer displays clips in different sizes based on their lengths (**Figure 8.6**).

- As editor, you have power over time. Clips can appear in any order, no matter when the events happened chronologically. (Most studio movies are rarely—if ever—shot in chronological order.)

- You can rearrange a movie's clips only in the Clip Viewer. The Timeline Viewer creates black frames if you try (see later in this chapter for more on black frames).

- If you need to determine when a clip was originally filmed, select it and look to the top of the Clip Viewer or Timeline Viewer. iMovie notes the date and time the clip was recorded (**Figure 8.6**).

Editing Clips

Remember in Chapter 2 when I advised you to shoot plenty of footage? Take a moment to look back on those lingering, leisurely days, because in this chapter you're going to chop your film into the smallest pieces you can, and still keep it comprehensible. Part of your job as editor is to arrange the many takes into a unified whole, but you also want to keep your audience awake.

iMovie offers four methods for editing clips: *splitting*, which divides a clip where the Playhead is located; *trimming*, which deletes a selection of frames; *cropping*, which deletes the frames that aren't selected; and *copying and pasting*, which creates a new clip based on selected frames. These actions can be performed on clips that are on the Shelf or in the Viewers.

Remember that you can use Undo to easily cancel up to the last 10 edits you've made. Also, you can always resurrect clips that have been cut up (see "Restoring Clips" at the end of this chapter).

To split a clip:

1. Position the Playhead at the point where you want to split the clip.

2. Choose Split Video Clip at Playhead from the Edit menu, or press Command-T. A new clip is created and placed next to the original (**Figure 8.7**). iMovie appends a slash and number to the name to indicate it's a partial clip (such as "Trees/1").

✔ Tips

■ This command works wherever the Playhead is located—you don't need to select a clip in order to split it.

■ After splitting, the two clips are still selected. To deselect the clips, click the top of the Viewer, or select another clip.

Single clip

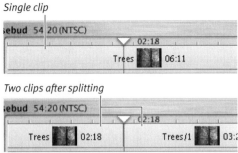

Two clips after splitting

Figure 8.7 Use the Split Video Clip at Playhead command to slice a clip into two separate clips.

Get In, Get Out

There are times when long, lingering shots can define a scene or even an entire movie—but not many. When you're editing, concentrate on making your movies *tight*, showing only the essential shots within your scenes. For example, it's a good idea to have an establishing shot of a room, and perhaps a person opening the door. But you don't need to show him closing the door, walking to the center of the room, and beginning a conversation. Jump right to the conversation, since that's probably the core action of the scene. This advice applies to all types of movies: for your trip to the zoo, jump straight to the lions; we don't need to see you bounce along the pathway looking for directions.

Of course, there are always exceptions (watching *2001: A Space Odyssey* immediately comes to mind), but a tighter film is almost always a better film.

Crop markers

Figure 8.8 The ghostly crop markers only appear when your pointer is below the scrubber bar.

Drag to make a selection

Figure 8.9 Click and drag to create a selection, which appears in yellow.

Right crop marker dragged past left one

Figure 8.10 Dragging one crop marker past the other swaps their positions (right becomes left, or left becomes right). This allows you to make a different selection in only one mouse move instead of several.

To select portions of a clip:

1. Position your pointer at the bottom of the scrubber bar; the crop markers appear (**Figure 8.8**).

2. Click and drag to make your selection, which is highlighted yellow (**Figure 8.9**). The Monitor playback follows your pointer so you can see the frames being selected.

   or

   Shift-click in the scrubber bar to make a selection.

3. Move the crop markers to fine-tune your selection.

✔ Tips

- Click on another clip or at the top of the Timeline Viewer to deselect the frames. You can also choose Select None from the Edit menu (Command-D).

- If you move the right crop mark past the left crop mark, it becomes the left mark (**Figure 8.10**). However, if you use the Shift-click method, the selection is extended in the direction based on which crop mark is closest.

- With a selection made on the scrubber bar, choose Select All from the Edit menu (or press Command-A) to highlight all the frames in the clip; conversely, choose Select None from the Edit menu (or press Command-D) to cancel your selection. This only works when you have a selection made; otherwise it selects or deselects all clips in your movie.

- The crop markers can be finicky at times. If you're positioning your pointer beneath the scrubber bar and not seeing the ghosted markers, try clicking and dragging anyway to force their appearance.

EDITING CLIPS

To trim a clip:

1. Select a portion of a clip.

2. Choose Clear or Cut from the Edit menu, or hit the Delete key. The selection is removed (**Figure 8.11**).

   If you chose to cut the selection, it will be stored in your Mac's Clipboard.

To crop a clip:

1. Select a portion of a clip.

2. Choose Crop from the Edit menu, or press Command-K. The selection is retained, and the rest of the clip's frames are deleted (**Figure 8.12**).

✔ Tip

- iMovie 2.1.1, released in September 2001, appears to have introduced a bug where cutting or clearing a section from the middle of a clip creates two separate clips representing the remaining footage, instead of removing a piece and keeping the clip whole.

Selection will be deleted.

Before trimming   *After trimming*

Figure 8.11 Trimming deletes selected frames, as indicated by the clip's duration before and after being trimmed.

Frames outside selection will be deleted.

Before cropping   *After cropping*

Figure 8.12 Cropping works opposite to trimming. The frames outside the selection are deleted.

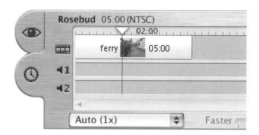

Pasted selection

Figure 8.13 When pasting a copied selection into your movie, the new clip splits any existing clip at the Playhead and pushes its parts out of the way.

Duplicated clip

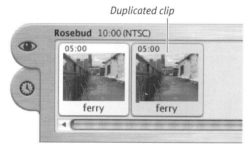

Figure 8.14 Duplicating a clip creates an exact clone of the original, which is why it's a good idea to rename the new clip.

To copy and paste a selection to a new clip:

1. Select a portion of a clip.

2. Choose Copy from the Edit menu, or press Command-C. The selection is stored in your Mac's Clipboard.

3. Select any clip on the Shelf, then choose Paste from the Edit menu (Command-V). iMovie creates a new clip.

   or

   Position the Playhead in your movie to the location where you want the clip to appear, then paste it. iMovie inserts the new clip at that point, splitting any clip that was present and pushing its remaining footage to the right (**Figure 8.13**).

To duplicate an entire clip:

1. Select the clip.

2. Choose Copy from the Edit menu.

3. Choose Paste from the Edit menu. A new, identical clip appears beside the original (**Figure 8.14**).

✔ Tips

- Consider renaming your new, pasted clip, since it will share the original's name.

- You can edit clips in this fashion in the Shelf, too. What's nice about doing it in the Clip Viewer or Timeline Viewer is that the new clips are already in your movie.

Pasting Clips over Clips

In addition to pasting a whole clip into your movie, which inserts it and pushes aside other footage, you can also replace a section of an existing clip (or clips). This is an easy way to show different visuals while retaining a clip's original audio, such as when someone is narrating a flashback (**Figure 8.15**). You can choose to make the sound of the pasted clip audible or silent.

To set the audio preference:

1. Open iMovie's Preferences and click the Advanced tab.

2. To retain the audio of the original clip, enable the Extract Audio in Paste Over option, if it's not already active (**Figure 8.16**). If you want to substitute in the audio of the pasted clip, disable Extract Audio in Paste Over. Click OK.

To paste a clip over another clip:

1. Select and cut or copy some footage or a clip.

2. Position the Playhead where you want the pasted footage to begin, or select a range of frames to be replaced.

3. Choose Paste Over at Playhead from the Advanced menu, or press Command-Shift-V. If you've selected a range of frames, the option reads Paste Over.

   The pasted clip appears directly on top of the clip that was there before, with its sound clip—colored orange—added to the first audio track (**Figure 8.17**). The audio clip actually belongs to the original clip, and is what you hear when you play the sequence. The clip you inserted still has its soundtrack embedded, but the volume is now turned off (see Chapter 9 for more on editing audio).

Figure 8.15 Using the Paste Over feature, you can add a flashback (middle) without interrupting the audio of your subject speaking.

Figure 8.16 To make sure the original clip's audio plays, enable the Extract Audio in Paste Over option.

Clip pasted over   Audio track from
at Playhead   original clip

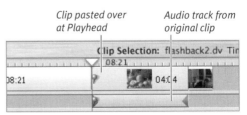

Figure 8.17 The pasted-over clip is rendered silent and the original clip's audio is extracted.

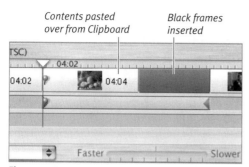

Contents pasted over from Clipboard   *Black frames inserted*

Figure 8.18 iMovie automatically adds black frames if the Clipboard contents are shorter than the selection in your movie.

Pasted over clip

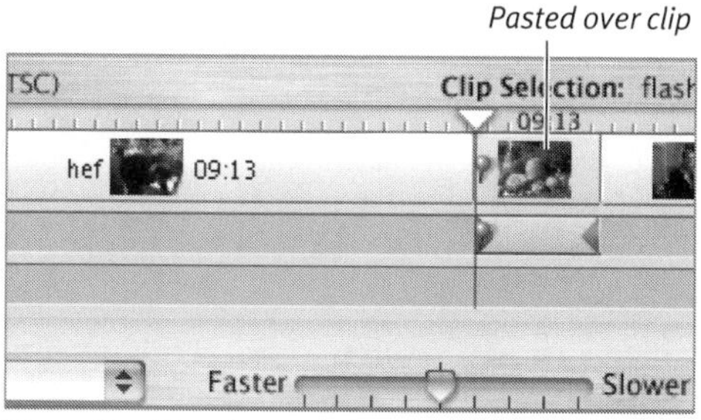

Figure 8.19 If you've made a selection in your movie that's shorter than the contents of the Clipboard, iMovie only pastes over as much as will fit.

✔ Tips

- Selecting a range of frames in the existing clip and then pasting over from the Clipboard can create a number of interesting results.

  If the number of frames in both clips matches exactly, the footage is added with no worries, mate.

  If the selection is longer than the footage on the Clipboard, black frames are added to make up the difference (**Figure 8.18**).

  If the selection is shorter than the footage on the Clipboard, iMovie pastes only as much footage as will fit into the selection (**Figure 8.19**).

- When you use the paste-over technique, you're actually overwriting the existing footage (versus overlaying something such as a title; see Chapter 11). This means that if you delete the pasted-over clip, you don't get the existing footage back. The only way to get the lost footage back is to use Undo, or completely restore the clip media (explained at the end of this chapter).

- If you're looking for a Robert Altman-esque audio effect where the audio from both clips is playing simultaneously, use Paste Over. Click the pasted clip (which retains its embedded audio track if the Extract Audio in Paste Over option is enabled), then increase its volume (see Chapter 9).

PASTING CLIPS OVER CLIPS

Reversing Clip Direction

Playing a clip backwards can be good for more than just comic value or special effects. This feature comes in handy more often than I ever thought: a clip played in reverse can sometimes blend better into the next scene (for example, zooming out of a landscape). Then again, I find it hard to resist tweaking reality by making a spilled glass of milk clean itself or coaxing waterfalls to rush *up*.

Reversed clip indicator

Figure 8.20 Look for this triangle icon to see which clips have been reversed.

To reverse clip direction:

1. Select a clip.

2. Choose Reverse Clip Direction from the Advanced menu, or press Command-R. A triangle icon appears on the clip to indicate that it's reversed (**Figure 8.20**).

   To restore the clip's direction later, simply choose Reverse Clip Direction again.

✔ Tips

■ Reversed clips feature backwards audio as well as visuals. You'll probably want to make the clip silent and play some other audio track in its place.

■ iMovie 2.1.1 and earlier includes a bug where cropping a reversed clip doesn't keep the correct range of frames. To crop a reversed clip, first set it to play normally, apply the crop, and then reverse it.

Normal speed   *Clip Speed slider*

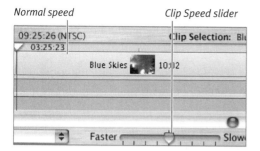

Twice as fast

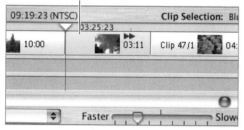

Super speedy

Figure 8.21 As you increase the Clip Speed slider, the clip shrinks to indicate how much time it occupies.

Sped-up clip

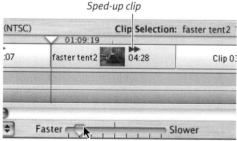

Figure 8.22 This clip has been sped up, exported to tape, re-imported into iMovie, and sped up again. You've never seen me move so fast.

Changing Playback Speed

Creating sped-up or slow-motion imagery used to involve changing a camera's shutter speed (the faster the film moved, the more individual pictures could be shot, creating slow motion, for example). In iMovie, all you have to do is move a slider.

To speed up or slow down video:

1. Select the clip you wish to alter in the Timeline Viewer.

2. Move the Clip Speed slider toward Faster (to speed up) or Slower (to slow down). The clip contracts or expands in the timeline to indicate its new duration as you move the slider (**Figure 8.21**).

iMovie's Clip Speed slider can make a clip five times faster or five times slower than the original speed. If you need a clip that's faster or slower than that, follow these steps.

To make clips super fast or super slow:

1. Speed up or slow down the footage in your movie as described above.

2. Export the footage to your camera's tape.

3. Re-import that footage into iMovie. Since it's regular footage now, iMovie considers its speed to be normal.

4. Use the Clip Speed slider to change the speed of the new clip (**Figure 8.22**).

✔ Tips

■ You can also simply click a portion of the slider's scale to adjust the speed, instead of moving the slider knob.

■ Changing clip speed is especially helpful on clips of scenery or backgrounds. Draw out scenes you shot too quickly, or speed up long pans to improve the pacing of your movie.

Creating a Still Clip

Thousands of still images flicker by as we're watching video—sometimes too quickly. Perhaps you'd like to linger on a sunset or highlight the one short moment when everyone in your family was looking at the camera. You can create a clip from a single frame of video, and specify its duration.

To create a still clip:

1. Position the Playhead at the frame you wish to use.

2. Choose Create Still Clip from the Edit menu, or press Command-Shift-S. A new 5-second clip appears, named "Still 03" (iMovie sets the number) (**Figure 8.23**).

To change a still clip's duration:

1. Select the still clip. Notice that the title area of the Clip Viewer or Timeline Viewer now includes an editable Time field (**Figure 8.24**).

2. Enter the duration you want. New clips are 5 seconds long, but you can change this default in iMovie's preferences.

To change the default still clip length:

1. Open iMovie's preferences.

2. Change the value in the field labeled Still Clips are [duration] seconds by default (**Figure 8.25**). Click OK.

   Changing the default won't update any existing clips—it will only affect new clips made after the change.

✔ Tip

■ When changing the duration in the Time field, enter the time quickly by selecting the whole field (press Command-A) and typing the total number of frames. So entering 3,000 gives you a 10-second clip (30 frames per second times 10).

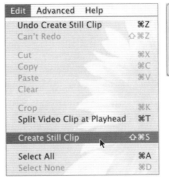

Figure 8.23 A new 5-second clip appears on the Shelf when you choose Create Still Clip.

Figure 8.24 When you click a still clip (whether it's on the Shelf or in your movie), you can change its duration in the Time field that appears.

Figure 8.25 If you create a lot of still clips, or you just don't like 5 seconds, change the still clip duration in iMovie's preferences.

Black frames added

Figure 8.26 Dragging a clip to the right adds a clip composed of black frames before it.

Black frames clip

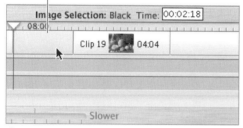

Figure 8.27 Click a black clip to display the Time field at the top of the Timeline Viewer, then edit the time.

Inserting Black Frames

When you add clips to your movie, they're inserted end to end without any gaps. But sometimes you want to start a clip at one specific point. While you're experimenting with the timing of your movie, you can insert placeholder clips consisting of black frames to pad sections of the movie.

To insert black frames:

1. In the Timeline Viewer, select the clip that immediately follows the section where you want to add black frames.

2. Click and drag the clip to the right. A black clip appears (**Figure 8.26**).

3. Continue dragging until the black clip is the duration you want.

   or

   After the black clip has been created, change its duration in the Time field of the Clip Viewer's or Timeline Viewer's title bar (**Figure 8.27**).

✔ Tips

- If there's a transition preceding the clip you need to move, you'll need to delete the transition first.

- Black-framed clips don't need to be just placeholders. If you need some black footage longer than what's available using a transition such as Fade In or Fade Out, for example, insert a black clip. You can even paste the clip over footage to keep the audio playing while the screen is dark (see "Pasting Clips over Clips" earlier in this chapter). Another benefit of this is that, unlike using black footage you shot with the camera, black clips don't occupy hard disk space.

Restoring Clips

It's not uncommon for me to chop up a single long clip into so many little pieces that I've lost track of where they are. Some thrown away (in a Trash I can't open), some trimmed and reversed, some on the Shelf, and even a few in the movie itself. So imagine my frustration when I realize that I *really* need about two seconds of footage from the beginning that is now scattered throughout my project. Is all that work gone?

No way. iMovie has a last-ditch method of getting it all back, thanks to the way it stores files. As I mentioned in Chapter 6, clips you create don't actually exist as new files on your hard disk. Instead, iMovie simply notes what changes have been applied to clips, and grabs the necessary information from the clip's original data file. Using the Restore Clip Media command, iMovie can recover the clip as it was when you first imported it.

To restore a clip:

1. Select a clip in your movie or on the Shelf that you want to restore.

2. Choose Restore Clip Media from the Advanced menu. A dialog box explains the amount of footage that will be restored (**Figure 8.28**).

3. Click Restore to restore, or Cancel to dismiss the dialog box.

✔ Tips

- I like to make a copy of an altered clip before I restore it, just in case I need that edited snippet again.

- If you've emptied the Trash, *you can't restore your clips.* As part of emptying the Trash, iMovie deletes the actual portions of the data files that have been deleted. So be certain you want to empty the Trash before you do it.

Figure 8.28 No matter how many times you chop up a clip in iMovie, the Restore Clip Media command is ready to pick up the pieces.

9

EDITING AUDIO

How important is audio in a movie? If you ever get the chance to attend an advance test screening of a Hollywood movie, the answer may be painfully clear. I've been to screenings where the audio in some scenes consisted of just what was recorded on set—no background music, no sound mixing to balance actors' voices and dampen background noise, no re-recorded dialogue to enhance enunciation. Although quite a bit of work goes into editing audio, people tend not to notice it unless something is wrong.

We covered some methods for capturing quality audio in Chapter 5, which is the first step. But audio can be much more than just video's underappreciated sibling. In this chapter, you'll see how editing audio tracks can give depth to your movie by working independently of the video, and by adding music, narration, and sound effects.

Changing a Clip's Volume

When you import footage, the video and audio are combined in the Timeline Viewer's video track (**Figure 9.1**). So as you're editing video clips, you're also editing the audio—splitting, trimming, and cropping it with the visuals. You can also control how loud an individual clip plays.

To set a clip's volume:

1. In the Timeline Viewer, select the clip you wish to edit.

2. Drag the volume control slider in the lower-right corner of the screen to the level you want (**Figure 9.2**).

✔ Tips

- You can't always control the sounds that surround you when you're filming. Sometimes unexpected background noises show up, or maybe someone closer to the camera's microphone was recorded louder than another person in the frame. In these cases, you can de-emphasize a sound. Split your clip right before and after the sound, then lower that small clip's volume (**Figure 9.3**). You may want to add some ambient noise in its place, so that the sound doesn't completely drop out, which we'll cover later this chapter.

- Unfortunately, iMovie lacks a precise way to measure sound, so it's difficult to match the sound level of another clip. I'd love to see an optional numeric readout. Instead, select the clips you want to match and then set a new sound level, which will be applied to each.

Video and audio data combined

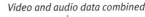

Figure 9.1 Although the top track is usually referred to as the video track, it also contains the clip's audio.

Volume control slider

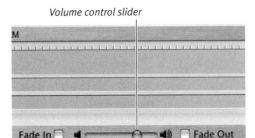

Figure 9.2 The volume control slider at the far right of the Timeline Viewer sets each clip's volume.

Selected clip

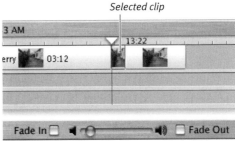

Figure 9.3 To de-emphasize audio, isolate the frames where it occurs by splitting the clip before and after the sound, then select the clip and lower its volume.

Fade Out checkbox

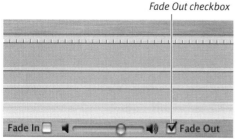

Figure 9.4 Use the Fade In and Fade Out checkboxes in the Timeline Viewer to apply iMovie's default audio fade duration of 01:14.

Figure 9.5 The Clip Info dialog box provides more control over the duration of audio fades.

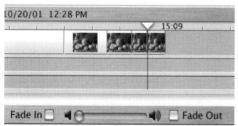

Figure 9.6 The longer clip above has been split into incrementally smaller clips, with each clip given a lower volume setting.

Fading Audio In or Out

Clips begin and end at specific times, which means the audio starts and stops abruptly. Using iMovie's audio fade controls, you can bring up or drop off the sound gradually.

To fade audio in or out:

1. Select a clip in the Timeline Viewer, the Clip Viewer, or the Shelf.

2. Click either the Fade In or Fade Out checkbox near the volume control slider (**Figure 9.4**). The fade duration is set to 01:14 by default.

To change the fade duration:

1. Open the Clip Info dialog box by either double-clicking a clip, or selecting it and choosing Get Clip Info from the File menu.

2. Click the Audio Fade In or Audio Fade Out checkbox.

3. Adjust the fade duration by moving the sliders (**Figure 9.5**).

✔ Tips

- When you apply a Fade In or Fade Out transition (see next chapter), the audio automatically fades to accompany the visual effect.

- If the Fade checkboxes include a hyphen when you select multiple clips, it means they have separate fade settings.

- Audio fades in iMovie hit the extremes of the scale: fading in starts at silence and ends at the audio level you've set for the clip, and fading out does the opposite. You can't fade from full volume to half volume, for example. If you're looking to bring the volume down part way, you can either edit the sound in another application (see Appendix D) or split your clip into several shorter clips whose volumes are incrementally lowered (**Figure 9.6**).

Extracting Audio

So far, I haven't mentioned the two obvious audio tracks that appear in the Timeline Viewer. These are typically where you would work with sound effects or imported audio files, but they're also the sandboxes for playing with audio that comes with your video footage. Before we can play, however, we need to extract the audio from the video clip.

To extract audio:

1. Select the clip in the video track.

2. Choose Extract Audio from the Advanced menu, or press Command-J. An audio clip, represented as an orange bar, appears in the audio track beneath the video clip (**Figure 9.7**).

✔ Tips

- If you later delete an extracted audio clip, it's not gone forever. The original sound is still embedded in the video track, but its volume is turned down to zero so it does not interfere with the audio tracks. If you can't undo the deletion, select the clip and increase its volume to restore the sound. You can then extract the audio again, which places a new copy in the audio track.

- Extracting audio clips makes it possible to start playing audio before the visuals begin (or after they're done). For example, when editing the video of a recent camping trip, I wanted to portray how it felt to wake up one morning to rain (**Figure 9.8**). I opened on a few seconds of black frames with the sound of the rain pattering on a tarp, then faded in on the image of the wet tarp. The audio and visuals weren't synchronized, but that didn't matter because the clip was an establishing shot with background sounds.

Extracted audio

Figure 9.7 Extracted audio clips appear on the first audio track and are colored orange.

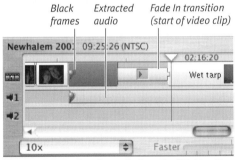

Black frames   Extracted audio   Fade In transition (start of video clip)

Figure 9.8 Extracting the audio from the "Wet tarp" clip allowed me to begin playing the sound of the rain during a few seconds of black frames, then fade in on the visual of the tarp itself (top). You can view this clip at www.peachpit.com/vqs/imovie/.

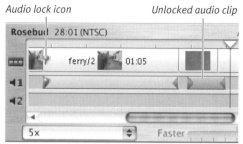

Figure 9.9 Once unlocked, you can position an audio clip anywhere in the movie. Here, the clip on the right is shifted out of sync with its video.

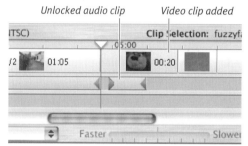

Figure 9.10 The unlocked audio clip gets pushed further out of sync when a new video clip is added.

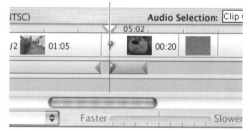

Figure 9.11 Choosing Lock Audio Clip at Playhead anchors the audio clip at a specific location.

Locking and Unlocking Audio Clips

After you extract an audio clip, it appears with a pushpin icon at its far left. This icon indicates that the video and audio tracks are synchronized, or locked, at that point. But you can unlock the clip, then drag it elsewhere on the timeline.

To unlock an audio clip:

1. Select the audio clip (not the video clip) in the Timeline Viewer. If you've just extracted the audio clip, it should be already selected.

2. Choose Unlock Audio Clip from the Advanced menu, or press Command-L. If you don't see this command, it means the audio clip isn't selected. The pushpin icon disappears (**Figure 9.9**).

Similarly, you can lock an extracted audio clip to any video clip in your movie. Locking it ensures that the sound remains synchronized, even if you add video clips later (**Figure 9.10**).

To lock an audio clip:

1. Position the audio clip where you want it to appear on the timeline.

2. Move the Playhead to a spot where the audio and video clips overlap (it doesn't have to be at the beginning).

3. Choose Lock Audio Clip at Playhead from the Advanced menu, or hit Command-L. A new pushpin icon appears at the Playhead location (**Figure 9.11**).

✔ Tip

■ Locking audio at the Playhead, instead of at the start of a clip, allows you to edit the video and audio clips without disrupting the synchronization.

Editing Audio Clips

When you extract audio, it becomes its own clip that you can edit independently of its original video clip.

To rename an audio clip:

1. Select the audio clip. You'll see a field in the Timeline Viewer's title bar called Audio Selection, which contains the name of the source video clip, such as "Samurai Kitty - Audio".

2. Highlight the text in that field and type in a new name (**Figure 9.12**).

3. Press Return to apply the change.

To split an audio clip:

1. Select the audio clip. Unlike video clips, which are split at the Playhead even if they're not selected, audio clips must be selected with the Playhead in place.

2. Choose Split Selected Audio Clip at Playhead from the Edit menu, or press Command-T (**Figure 9.13**).

Changing a clip's duration

Video clips use crop markers on the scrubber bar to select a range of frames. Audio clips, by contrast, feature crop markers at each end of the clip that determine at what point a clip becomes audible and when it goes silent. Simply drag the triangular crop markers to change the clip's duration (**Figure 9.14**). The highlighted section between the markers (which appears as a somewhat brighter orange when the clip is not selected) is what will be heard during playback.

If you prefer, you can leave the rest of the clip dangling in case you need to adjust the clip's duration in the future. However, this can lead to overlapping clips that are difficult to select. If you're satisfied with the clip's length, you can crop out the unused sections.

Figure 9.12 Selecting an audio clip activates the Audio Selection field, where you can rename the clip.

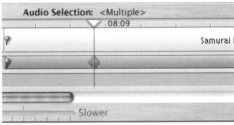

Figure 9.13 You can split an extracted audio clip without splitting the video clip to which it's attached.

Audible portion of clip

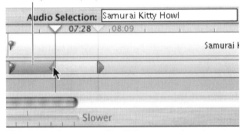

Figure 9.14 Drag an audio clip's crop markers to set which portion will be audible during playback.

Audio clip cropped

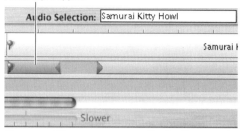

Figure 9.15 When you crop an audio clip, the unused portions are removed, not just kept silent.

Last video clip

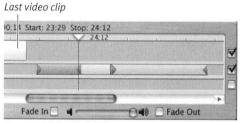

Figure 9.16 The end of your movie is a convenient location to temporarily store unused audio clips.

Audio clip   *Fade Out would occur here.*

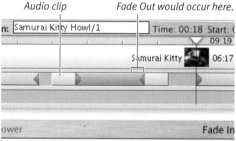

Figure 9.17 Audio fades begin and end where the crop markers are located, not at the start or end of a clip.

To crop an audio clip:

1. Set a clip's crop markers to your liking.

2. Choose Crop from the Edit menu, or press Command-K. The unused portions are removed (**Figure 9.15**).

✔ Tips

- Clips can go into either audio track in the Timeline Viewer, though iMovie tends to use the second track for imported audio.

- Although audio clips act like video clips in most respects, you can only edit them in the Timeline Viewer; there's no audio equivalent to the Shelf. However, you can temporarily store audio clips you aren't yet using: simply drag them beyond the end of the last video track (**Figure 9.16**).

- You don't have to select an audio clip before you adjust its crop markers. Grabbing a marker selects the clip for you.

- Audio is notoriously difficult to trim to the right length. Fine-tune your editing by using the left and right arrow keys: selecting a clip anywhere in the middle moves the entire clip when the keys are pressed, while clicking once on either crop marker makes it respond to your key presses.

- Unlike video clips, audio clips can overlap (though this can create audible gibberish, but that may be what you're going for).

- If you adjust an audio clip's duration using its crop markers, any fades you apply are calculated based on the clip's start and stop times, not by the actual beginning or ending of the clip (**Figure 9.17**).

- Experiment with overlapping clips that contain fades. This is an easy way to blend dialogue, for example (one quickie method for playing voices in a character's head), or even tighten scenes by reducing the amount of lag between speakers.

Sound Effects

You can't capture *every* sound when you're shooting—the laser blasts in *Star Wars* weren't real, for example (they were actually recordings of wrenches striking power cables). Sometimes you need ready-made sound effects (a few are included with iMovie), or even create your own.

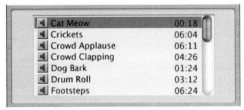

Figure 9.18 iMovie includes a number of common sound effects that you can add to your movie.

To add a sound effect to your movie:

1. Switch to iMovie's Audio panel. A list of effects appears in the top portion (**Figure 9.18**).

2. Click an effect's name to preview it (but don't click Wagon Crash if you're wearing headphones—ouch!).

3. Drag the effect you want to the Timeline Viewer and drop it into one of the audio tracks. It appears as two connected squares occupying the duration of the clip (**Figure 9.19**).

   You can move sound effects, as well as control their playback volume and apply fades, but you can't change their lengths or split them like other audio clips.

Sound effect start   *Sound effect end*

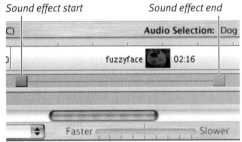

Figure 9.19 A sound effect's duration is indicated by a line connecting the two ends of the effect.

✔ Tip

■ Kudos to Apple's engineers: iMovie automatically displays the Timeline Viewer when you start dragging a sound effect.

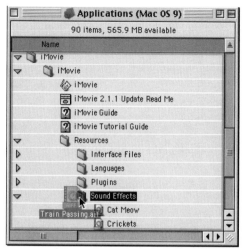

Figure 9.20 Sound effects in Mac OS 9 are stored in the Resources folder, located in iMovie's application folder.

Additional iMovie files go here under Mac OS X.

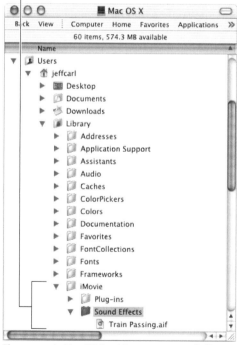

Figure 9.21 In Mac OS X, add your own sound effects to the iMovie folder within your user Library folder.

To add new sound effects to iMovie:

1. Quit iMovie.

2. Make sure the sound file is in the AIFF format. A number of utilities, such as Apple's QuickTime Pro Player, can convert sound formats (see Appendix D for more information).

3. In Mac OS 9, copy the sound file to iMovie's Sound Effects folder, located in the Resources folder within the iMovie folder (**Figure 9.20**).

   If you're using Mac OS X, go to your Home directory, or open the Users folder, then the folder with your name. Open the Library folder, and then the iMovie folder (if there is no iMovie folder, go ahead and create one). Finally, copy the sound file to the Sound Effects folder (again, if one doesn't exist, go ahead and create one) (**Figure 9.21**).

4. Launch iMovie. The sound is now listed in the Audio panel.

✔ Tips

- A broad assortment of audio clips are available. Apple lists some you can download (www.apple.com/imovie/freestuff/), and there are many companies that sell or license audio libraries. See Appendix D for a list of where to begin looking.

- Don't go overboard with adding sound effects to iMovie's library: the more items, the longer it takes iMovie to launch.

- A cheap and easy way to create your own sound effects is to record them in iMovie using the narration feature (see "Recording Voice-overs" later in this chapter).

SOUND EFFECTS

Grabbing Music from an Audio CD

Nearly every movie—studio pictures, home-made shorts, television commercials—uses background music. iMovie includes the capability to extract songs from any music CD you put into your Mac and turn them into editable audio clips.

To extract a song from an audio CD:

1. Insert the audio CD into your Mac's CD or DVD drive.

2. Click the Audio button in iMovie to bring up the Audio panel. If a CD is present, its tracks appear in the panel.

3. Drag a song title from the Audio panel to the position in the timeline where you want it to begin playing (**Figure 9.22**). iMovie normally uses track 2, but you can drag the song to either track.

   The extracted track appears as a purple audio clip, and can be edited like other audio clips (**Figure 9.23**).

✔ Tip

■ Audio CDs typically don't contain descriptive information such as song titles or artists, so you end up with a list of songs named "Track 01," "Track 02," and the old-time favorite, "Track 03." Using a program such as Apple's iTunes, however, your Mac can access the CDDB database, a vast collection of online album and song information that coincides with an album's unique identifier (**Figure 9.24**). Mac OS 9 stores this information on your hard disk for future reference (and access by other programs, such as iMovie); however, iMovie 2.1.1 under Mac OS X 10.1 (the current versions as of this writing) can't access that data, so titles remain decidedly unat-"Track"-tive.

Figure 9.22 When you insert an audio CD into your Mac's media drive, the track list appears in iMovie. Simply drag a track name to the timeline to copy it from the CD.

Audio track from CD

Figure 9.23 Tracks added from a CD show up as purple audio clips.

Figure 9.24 iTunes can automatically consult the online CDDB database of album and song titles.

Audio CD 43:55:00
Track 01 04:00:00
Track 02 04:48:00
Track 03 04:07:00
Track 04 03:11:00
Track 05 04:53:00
Track 06 04:14:00
Track 07 03:14:00
Track 08 04:51:00
Track 09 02:01:00
Track 10 03:57:00
Track 11 04:34:00

Record Music

Figure 9.25 Click the Play button to begin listening to the selected audio track.

Audio CD 43:55:00
Track 01 04:00:00
Track 02 04:48:00
Track 03 04:07:00
Track 04 03:11:00
Track 05 04:53:00
Track 06 04:14:00
Track 07 03:14:00
Track 08 04:51:00
Track 09 02:01:00
Track 10 03:57:00
Track 11 04:34:00

Record Music

Figure 9.26 When you've found the selection of music you want, click the Record Music button.

To extract a portion of a song:

1. With a CD in the drive and the Audio panel visible, position the Playhead at the point in your movie where you want the music to begin.

2. In the Audio panel, use the Play button to find a section of music you'd like to import (**Figure 9.25**). Unfortunately, you don't have a Playhead-type controller here, so you need to listen to the song in real time.

3. When you've found your song snippet, click the Record Music button (**Figure 9.26**). Your movie begins playing, and a purple audio clip appears in track 2 of the timeline. Clicking the Pause button puts both movie and music playback on hold; clicking it again resumes playback.

4. Click the Stop button to end recording. You can now edit the music clip like any other audio clip.

✔ Tips

- iMovie saves extracted songs as AIFF formatted files. If you're going to be grabbing lots of little clips, you're better off using iTunes to locate those sections and save them as AIFF files (in iTunes's preferences, switch to the Importing tab and select AIFF Encoder from the Import Using popup menu). You can then import the clips into iMovie (see "Importing Audio Files," later in this chapter).

- It's worth pointing out that nearly anything you extract from an audio CD is probably copyrighted material. For most people this is no problem, since only friends and family are likely to see their edited movies. But if you're planning to distribute the movie or play it for large numbers of people, you'll need to get permission to use the music.

GRABBING MUSIC FROM AN AUDIO CD

Recording Voice-overs

I read that while shooting *Crouching Tiger, Hidden Dragon*, actor Chow Yun Fat (who doesn't speak Mandarin Chinese natively) didn't put much work into pronouncing his dialogue correctly while shooting. Instead, he fine-tuned his accent when re-recording the dialogue in post production. Most likely you won't be doing much re-recording (also called *looping*), but iMovie's narration capability lets you add voice-overs or other sounds directly to your movie.

To record a voice-over:

1. Connect a microphone to your Mac, if necessary.

2. Click the Audio button in iMovie to display the Audio panel.

3. Position the Playhead in the timeline where you want to begin recording.

4. Click the Record Voice button to begin recording; the button reads Stop while recording (**Figure 9.27**). The indicator above the button lights up according to the sound level.

5. Click the Stop button to end. A new audio clip, which can be edited just like other audio clips, is now in the timeline (**Figure 9.28**).

✔ Tips

- iMovie automatically stops recording after 5 minutes.

- You can record multiple takes, then delete the ones you don't end up using.

- Many of Apple's current computers don't include a microphone port, unfortunately. Instead, consider buying a USB audio device such as Griffin Technology's iMic (www.griffintechnology.com/).

Sound level indicator

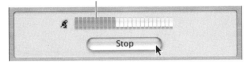

Figure 9.27 As you're recording a voice-over, the Record Voice button becomes the Stop button.

Voice-over recording

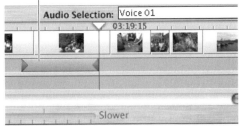

Figure 9.28 The recorded voice-over appears in the Timeline Viewer as a regular audio clip, named "Voice 01" (or whichever number applies).

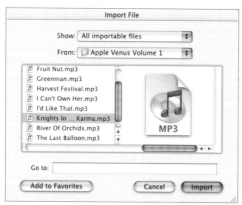

Figure 9.29 Mac OS X's Import File dialog box is a bit different from the one found in Mac OS 9, but the idea is the same: locate the MP3 file to add to your movie.

MP3 file added at Playhead

Figure 9.30 iMovie automatically places imported audio files into track 2 in the Timeline Viewer.

Importing Audio Files

As I mentioned earlier when talking about sound effects, there are many companies that provide royalty-free music and audio clips. iMovie can import files that are in MP3 and AIFF formats.

This capability actually becomes more attractive with MP3 files. You may want to import MP3 songs instead of grabbing them from an audio CD: MP3s occupy much less disk space than AIFF files, without a noticeable loss of quality, and you can more easily get MP3 music that isn't available on CD (from Web sites such as MP3.com).

To import an audio file:

1. Position the Playhead in the Timeline Viewer where you want the imported file to begin.

2. Choose Import File from the File menu, or press Command-I.

3. In the dialog box that appears, navigate to the audio file (**Figure 9.29**). Click Import.

4. Wait several seconds for the file to be imported, then be amazed when it shows up as an editable audio clip in the time-line's track 2 (**Figure 9.30**).

10

TRANSITIONS

Transitions can be equally wonderful and terrible things. They can move you from one scene to another without the abruptness of a straightforward cut, or help define a movie's pace by easing you gently into or out of a scene.

But transitions can also become a distraction, because you're introducing motion or visuals that weren't recorded by the camera. Too many transitions can be like using too many fonts in a word processing application: pretty soon, all you see is the style, not the content.

My best advice is to let the content determine the transition, if one is even needed: most of the time, a jump cut (moving from one clip to another without a transition) is all that's required. I'm not saying you should skip this chapter—rather, using fewer, *better* transitions is almost always the better route.

What's really pertinent at this stage is that iMovie creates professional transitions without breaking a sweat, enabling you to concentrate on how your movie plays instead of trying to jump over technical hurdles.

This chapter covers how to apply and modify transitions. To view a gallery of transitions iMovie offers (including Apple's downloadable Plug-in Pack), see Appendix A.

Editing Transition Settings

Clicking the Transitions button displays the Transitions panel, where you can preview the different effects and adjust their duration.

To preview a transition:

◆ Click a transition name. The preview window automatically plays a rough version of the transition (**Figure 10.1**).

◆ Click the Preview button to view the rough transition in the Monitor (**Figure 10.2**). Note that it will play slower than normal.

To change a transition's duration:

1. Select a transition, either in the Transition panel's list or one that you've already added to the movie.

2. Drag the Speed slider. The duration appears in the lower-right corner of the preview window (**Figure 10.3**). Transitions can be as short as 10 frames or as long as 4 seconds.

✔ Tips

■ To stop a preview, simply click elsewhere on the screen.

■ In general, iMovie creates a preview based on the location of the Playhead. If it's near the beginning of the clip, iMovie transitions the previous clip into the current one; if the Playhead is near the end of a clip, it transitions the current clip to the next clip. I say "in general," however, because the program isn't always consistent. Sometimes placing the Playhead at the start of the movie makes a transition between the first frames and then a section later in that clip. Try repositioning the Playhead and clicking a transition name again. As a last resort, you can add a transition, preview it, and use Undo if you don't like the result.

Figure 10.1 Clicking a transition name previews its effect in the Transition panel's preview window.

Figure 10.2 You can view a full-size, though rough, version of a transition in the Monitor.

Figure 10.3 The current Speed slider setting is shown in the corner of the preview window.

Push right.

Push down

Figure 10.4 The Push transition is the only one that features a directional control, at least for now.

Figure 10.5 Use Overlap to slowly dissolve from a clip to a modified still image.

Figure 10.6 GeeThree's Slick plug-ins for iMovie greatly expand your options for applying transitions.

To set an effect's direction:

1. Select the Push transition for an example of this type of setting. Although Push is the only Apple transition to use a directional control, the door is open for other developers to use it too.

2. Click a button on the directional control to specify how the effect plays (**Figure 10.4**). Using Push, the control indicates where the old clip exits the frame and the new clip enters (by default, the new clip "pushes" the old clip from left to right).

✔ Tips

- Transitions can also blend between movie footage and still clips. For example, you're editing an interview and you want to dissolve to an embarrassing high school photo of the interviewee. You can also achieve some low-tech special effects: suppose you want to end your video with a still image overlaid with styled text. Save one frame as a still image (explained in Chapter 7), and add the text in Photoshop or a similar program. Then, import the changed still image, and add a Cross Dissolve or Overlap transition before it (**Figure 10.5**).

- Apple has built into iMovie the most commonly used types of transitions, but you may be looking for a different kind of effect. If so, check out the Slick volumes of iMovie transitions and plug-ins developed by GeeThree, Inc. Although I can't honestly say I'll ever use the Heart transition, I like the subtlety of the Fog effects (**Figure 10.6**). You can preview each type of transition at the GeeThree Web site (www.geethree.com).

EDITING TRANSITION SETTINGS

Adding Transitions

Like so many things in iMovie, adding a transition to your movie is as easy as dragging and dropping an icon. The trickery (and I use the term loosely) is in configuring how it appears in the movie. Don't worry about nailing it the first time, though: you can always change a transition's settings, even after you've added it to your movie.

To add a transition:

Drag the transition to the intersection of two clips in the Clip Viewer or Timeline Viewer. (Transitions can be added to the beginning and end of the movie as well.) A transition icon appears, containing a red line moving from left to right (**Figure 10.7**).

That line indicates iMovie's progress of rendering the transitions. To build a transition, iMovie recreates the affected frames of the clip with the transition applied. For example, if we add a Fade In transition that's 1 second (30 frames) in duration, iMovie redraws each frame with a different brightness setting (**Figure 10.8**). This ensures that in the final movie, the transition appears at its best resolution and plays smoothly.

✔ Tips

■ Leave enough padding in your clips to accommodate transitions. Otherwise, iMovie displays an error that one or both of the clips is too short (**Figure 10.9**).

■ To cancel a transition while it's rendering, choose Undo from the Edit menu or press Command-period (.).

■ Go ahead and continue working while a transition is rendering, or even add other transitions, which are rendered concurrently. You can also play your movie before the rendering finishes, though the unrendered clips will appear jumpy and rough until they're done.

Rendering progress bar   *Transition icon*

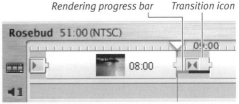

Figure 10.7 Transitions need to render before they can play back smoothly in the Monitor.

Figure 10.8 Transitions recreate your footage with the transition effect applied. Here are three frames from a Fade In transition.

This clip needs more footage if you want to add a transition after it (and avoid the error below).

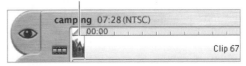

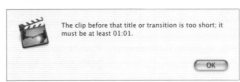

Figure 10.9 iMovie needs a certain amount of source material to work with. It will tell you how much footage is needed, based on your Speed slider setting.

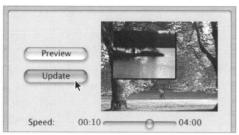

Figure 10.10 If you change a transition's settings, click the Update button to re-render it.

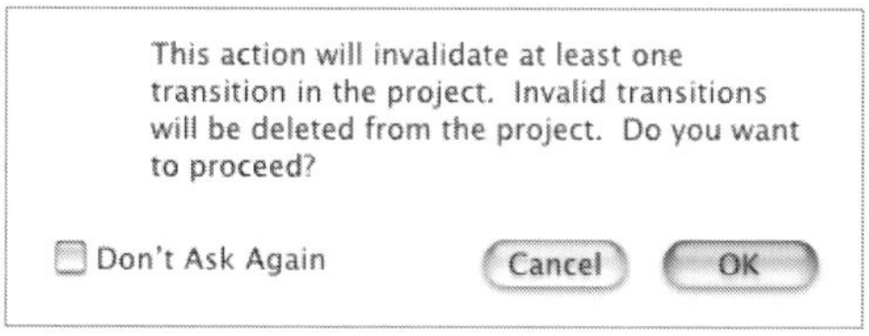

This action will invalidate at least one transition in the project. Invalid transitions will be deleted from the project. Do you want to proceed?

☐ Don't Ask Again   Cancel   OK

Figure 10.11 Don't say you weren't warned about moving a transition out of place. Then again, if you click the Don't Ask Again checkbox, you can say you weren't warned—but you won't get any sympathy from me. Well, all right, maybe a little sympathy. But this is the last time, got it? Okay? Good.

To modify existing transitions:

1. Select the transition in the Clip Viewer or Timeline Viewer.

2. Adjust the transition's settings in the Transitions panel.

3. Click the Update button to re-render the transition (**Figure 10.10**).

✔ Tips

■ Since transitions become their own clips, you can edit their volume levels, including fading in and out, just like other clips. The Fade In and Fade Out transitions automatically apply audio fades.

■ When you update a transition, most of the time you're adjusting the clip's duration. However, you can also change the type of transition entirely: just click your transition clip, select a new transition from the list, and click Update.

■ In the Clip Viewer, you might think you can pick up a transition and move it to another clip because the surrounding clips move aside when you drag the icon. However, all you get instead is an error warning you that your foolhardy action will delete the transition (**Figure 10.11**).

iMovie's Habit of Stealing Time

As you add transitions, you may notice something odd happening: your movie is getting *shorter*. Is it possible to add things to a movie and still end up with less than what you started? (And if so, does it apply to eating ice cream?)

Yes. (But no to the ice cream.) Here's what's happening (**Figure 10.12**):

How iMovie steals time using transitions

1. For the sake of not straining my math abilities, let's assume we want to add a Cross Dissolve transition between two 10-second clips. The clips contain outside shots of a lake and some trees, so in order to maintain a comfortable pace, we decide to make our transition 2 seconds long.

2. We drag the transition into place between the clips, and notice that each clip has become 8 seconds in length, not 9 seconds (to split a 2-second transition between two clips leaves 1 second for each clip: $10 - 1 = 9$).

3. The mystery is solved when we look at how iMovie is building the transition. It needs to start dissolving one clip into the other clip at the very beginning of the transition, so iMovie merges 2 seconds of *each* clip, removing 4 seconds total. The transition is still 2 seconds in duration, but required 4 seconds to perform the blends. Think of it as tightening a belt: you still have the same amount of material, but the overlap where the buckle rests allows you to encompass a smaller area.

Watching iMovie grab and modify clips is also the best motivation for locking any audio clips you've extracted (see Chapter 9). It only takes one transition to throw the rest of your movie out of sync.

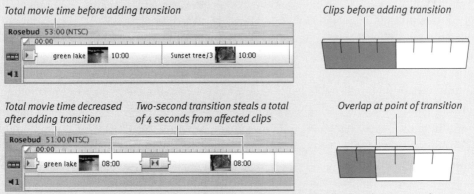

Total movie time before adding transition

Clips before adding transition

Total movie time decreased after adding transition   *Two-second transition steals a total of 4 seconds from affected clips*

Overlap at point of transition

Figure 10.12 Some transitions, such as Cross Dissolve, need to overlap two clips in order to merge the number of frames needed for the effect. This creates a shorter overall movie.

Before   *Transition*

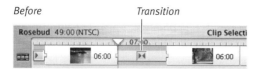

After

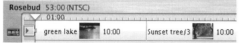

Figure 10.13 A transition acts like a regular clip most of the time, but when you delete it, the pieces of footage it used are returned to the nearby clips.

Figure 10.14 Using several Fade In and Fade Out transitions, these two images appear to display, then disappear quickly and smoothly (the QuickTime version is a better representation, believe me).

Most Valuable Transitions

In most situations, you'll find yourself using only a handful of transitions: Fade In, Fade Out, Cross Dissolve, and Overlap. I'm also partial to Wash In and Wash Out, in the right context. The others, to me, are usually too flashy for regular use.

One of the best uses of the subtle Fade In and Fade Out transitions is to pair them back to back to intercut a series of short scenes or still images: the picture goes from black to full strength (Fade In), runs for a second or two (or even shorter), then dissolves to black again (Fade Out), only to start again with a different scene (**Figure 10.14**). See an example at www.peachpit.com/vqs/imovie/.

Removing Transitions

Think of transitions as clips that are placed on top of the video track, rather than wedged between the other clips. This enables you to delete them without worrying that you're destroying any underlying footage.

To delete a transition:

1. Select the transition in the Clip Viewer or Timeline Viewer.

2. Press the Delete key, or choose Cut or Clear from the Edit menu. The sections of clips that were used by the transition are restored (**Figure 10.13**).

TITLES

In Hollywood, movie titles aren't mere words that flash up on the screen. Actors, agents, and studio executives negotiate for the length of time a person's name appears, how large or small the typeface is, whether the name comes before or after the movie title, and all sorts of other conditions that inflame my natural aversion to fine print. Hopefully, you won't deal with any of that, because the other aspects of movie titles—i.e., actually creating them—are made extraordinarily easy in iMovie.

The program's title capabilities are more robust than one would think, though I'll admit I'd like to see more typographic control in future versions. In the meantime, use the titling features with the knowledge that, as with a lot of iMovie capabilities, you're creating elements quickly and cheaply that used to cost a fortune for studios and filmmakers.

Editing the Text

Obviously, you'll need some text in your title. iMovie offers three types of text fields, depending on the type of title used. To begin editing titles, click the Titles button on the Shelf (**Figure 11.1**). As with transitions and effects, a rough example of each title plays in the preview window when clicked, and you can view a larger approximation in the Monitor by clicking the Preview button.

Text fields

Most of the title options use a set of two text fields. The top field typically acts as the primary title and appears larger in some titles than the bottom field.

To add text to title fields:

1. Click once within a field to select its contents. Click again to position the pointer.

2. Type new title text, then press Return or click outside the field (**Figure 11.2**).

Multiple text fields

If a two-line title isn't long enough, some titles offer multiple text fields, which are one or more field pairs. Usually, the extra fields are used for animating the text—for example, the Centered Multiple title displays the first field pair, clears the title, then displays the next field pair. Multiple fields are also used to set up titles, such as Rolling Credits, which face each other across the screen (**Figure 11.3**). You can add more text pairs and change their order, if you like.

To add text fields:

1. With a title selected that offers multiple text field pairs, click the plus-sign button. A new pair is created (**Figure 11.4**).

2. Type your text into the fields and press Return or click outside the field.

Figure 11.1 The Titles panel contains more controls than anything else in iMovie—and it's still easy.

Figure 11.2 Once you type your title into the text fields, you don't need to type it in again when switching between title styles.

Figure 11.3 Multiple text fields enable you to create titles with opposing elements, such as Rolling Credits.

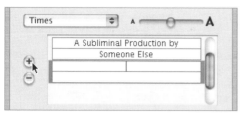

Figure 11.4 In title styles with multiple text fields, use the plus-sign button to add more fields.

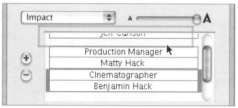

Figure 11.5 Think your name needs to appear sooner in the credits? Click and drag the text field into place.

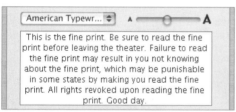

Figure 11.6 Text blocks let you enter more text than is allowed in other text fields.

To remove text fields:

1. Click a text pair to select it.

2. Click the minus-sign button. The pair is deleted.

To rearrange text fields:

1. Click a text pair to select it.

2. Drag the selection up or down the list to change its position, then drop it in place (**Figure 11.5**).

Text blocks

If you still need more text in your title, use a style with a text block field. It accommodates more text and can wrap your words (i.e., move them to the next line) as space allows.

To add text to block fields:

1. Type your text into the field.

   or

   Paste some text you've copied elsewhere, such as from a word processing application (**Figure 11.6**).

2. Click outside the field or press Enter to apply the text. (Unlike the other text fields in iMovie, pressing the Return key in a text block creates a line break instead of applying the edit.)

✔ Tips

■ You can select (and therefore delete or move) only one text pair at a time.

■ iMovie remembers the last text you entered, so you don't need to type it again if you click another title effect—or even if you create a new project.

EDITING THE TEXT

Editing Text Style

Now that you've entered some text, it's time
to give it style: select a color and a font,
change the type size, and optionally view the
title on a black background. The title controls are also particularly important if you're
planning to export the movie into
QuickTime format.

To select text color:

1. Click the square Color field below the
titles list in the Titles panel. A palette
containing 24 colors and eight shades of
gray appears (**Figure 11.7**).

2. Click a color to select it. You can try as
many colors as you like while the palette
is visible, and see them applied to text in
the preview window.

3. Click outside the palette to accept the
last color you applied.

To specify font and size:

1. Choose a font from the Title Font popup
menu.

2. Drag the Title Text Size slider to increase
or decrease the type size (**Figure 11.8**).

✔ Tips

■ The color control affects the color of the
text itself, except in the case of Stripe
Subtitle, where the color setting applies
to the text's background stripe.

■ To ensure that fonts appear smooth in
titles, use Adobe PostScript, TrueType, or
OpenType fonts. These include the fonts
included with the Mac OS. Don't use
bitmap fonts, which contain only enough
data to draw their letters onscreen in a
few specific sizes.

Figure 11.7 Use the popup selector to change the
color of your text. Click outside the palette to accept
the new color.

Figure 11.8 I'd really prefer a more specific way of
setting the font size, but the method used by the
Title Text Size slider is easier to comprehend.

Figure 11.9 Both of these titles were made using the
same font at the largest setting.

Over Black enabled

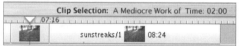

Over Black disabled

Figure 11.10 When the Over Black option is enabled (top), the text clip that's created doesn't incorporate the next clip's footage (middle). When Over Black is turned off, the text clip uses the next clip's footage (bottom) as background for the title.

QT Margins off

QT Margins on

Figure 11.11 QT Margins uses every available bit of space to render titles, running the risk of the words getting cut off when viewed on a TV.

Figure 11.12 Use a still image as background for your titles to add texture or set a mood for the movie.

- The longer your title, the smaller it appears, regardless of the font size you've specified (**Figure 11.9**).

To display text against a black background:

Click the Over Black checkbox. When you apply the style to the movie, it pushes aside the clips that follow it, rather than incorporate footage from the movie (**Figure 11.10**). Make sure any extracted audio clips are locked in place before you add a title with Over Black enabled.

Setting QuickTime margins

Remember toward the beginning of the book when I advised that you know in what format your movie will end up? Here's a chance to put that advice to the test. If you know the movie will only appear in QuickTime format, enable QT Margins, which uses more of the video area for titles (**Figure 11.11**). If you're exporting your movie back to tape to play it on a television, turn QT Margins off or your text might run outside the screen's edges.

✔ Tips

- If you don't use the Over Black option, your title appears over your footage. What if you want something different? Consider importing images that can be used as backdrop for your titles (**Figure 11.12**). You can use your own, or check out the selection of background sets that Apple offers for free (www.apple.com/imovie/freestuff/).

- The text style settings apply to every title effect listed in the Title panel. When I'm creating a title, I'll play with five or six options before settling on one, so it's nice that I don't need to enter the settings each time I click a title.

EDITING TEXT STYLE

Setting Title Duration

If we were dealing with still images, our work here would be done. But video is about movement, so don't expect titles to just flash onscreen and then disappear. Almost every iMovie title is animated in some way, which means you need to control how it moves. iMovie has two methods of doing this: the speed of the effect, and the length of the pause following the effect.

To set a title's duration:

1. Drag the Speed slider to specify how long it takes to complete the title's effect. The times vary between titles (**Figure 11.13**).

2. Drag the Pause slider to specify how long the titles remain onscreen after the title animation has finished. Some effects, such as Subtitle, don't offer a pause option. The combined times are shown in the preview window, indicating the total time of the title clip (**Figure 11.14**).

✔ Tips

- Some titles' speeds vary depending on what you've typed into the text fields. The Flying Letters title, for example, needs more time if there are more letters, which is why the maximum Speed setting changes for long titles (after typing your title, click another title, then click Flying Letters again to see the difference).

- Remember that not everyone may be able to read as fast as you. Give your viewers plenty of time to read your title—without boring them, of course.

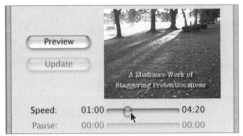

Figure 11.13 The Speed slider dictates the duration of a title effect's animation.

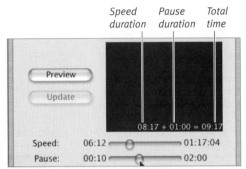

Figure 11.14 The Pause slider controls how long the title remains onscreen once the effect is finished. Dragging the slider updates the total time of the effect, as shown in the preview window.

Figure 11.15 The directional controller on some title effects determines which way the words appear onscreen.

Figure 11.16 Music Video gives you a little more control over text positioning because it's a block title.

Setting Title Position

Some effects, such as Bounce In To Center, feature a control for placing text on the screen or specifying the direction in which the text animates.

To set title position:

1. Click the title you wish to use.

2. Click an arrow on the directional controller to the left of the title list (**Figure 11.15**).

✔ Tip

■ The Music Video title gives you the option of running text along the left or right sides of the screen. But it's also a text block title, which means you can type line breaks (using Return). If you put the two features together, you can position text in the upper-left or right corners of the screen (**Figure 11.16**).

Adding Titles

Once you've decided how your title will look, you're ready to add it to your movie.

To add a title:

Drag and drop the title's name or icon to the left of the clip onto which it will appear (**Figure 11.17**). iMovie begins rendering the title in a new clip and names it with the start of the title's text.

Title clip rendering

When a title is rendered, iMovie actually writes the pixels to your footage, rather than generating them on the fly (such as when you preview a title's style). And like transitions and effects, titles render as their own clips. You can continue to work or play your movie while the title is rendering, though the playback won't be as smooth.

If a title clip is longer than the clip it's being applied to, the title clip runs on into the next clip (**Figure 11.18**).

✔ Tips

- Add multiple titles to the same section of footage by applying titles to a section of footage that already contains a title. For example, you can use the Drifting title to gradually display a scene's location, and add a Typewriter title in the middle of the Drifting clip that shows the time of day (you'll need to split the Drifting clip when it's done rendering before you can add the Typewriter clip) (**Figure 11.19**).

- When a title is generated, iMovie creates a new file on your hard disk called "Title 1" (or similar) that contains the rendered footage—but the original untitled clip is still intact. Be aware that using lots of titles can increase the amount of hard disk space used by your project.

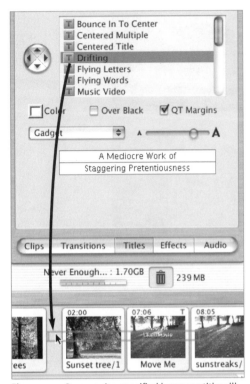

Figure 11.17 Once you've specified how your title will appear, drag and drop it onto the Clip Viewer or Timeline Viewer.

Before

| 1:28 | 06:11 | 02:00 | 04:17 |
| Black | Trees | Sunset tree/1 | sunstreaks |

After   *Title stole footage from next clip.*

| 1:28 | 06:11 | 03:05 T | 03:12 |
| Black | Trees | Move Me | sunstreaks |

Figure 11.18 The title is 03:05 in length, so putting it in front of a clip that's 02:00 causes the title to grab footage from the next clip.

Figure 11.19 Combine multiple titles by applying a new title effect to an existing one.

Figure 11.20 The Update button becomes active if you select a clip with a title applied. Change its settings and click Update to re-render the clip.

Modifying and Deleting Existing Titles

When you add a title clip, it actually exists on top of your footage. If you don't like the way it turned out, you can easily change its properties, or get rid of it altogether.

To modify an existing title:

1. Select the title clip.

2. Make any changes you wish in the Titles panel.

3. Click the Update button to apply your changes (**Figure 11.20**).

To remove a title:

1. Select the offending title clip.

2. Press the Delete key. You can also drag the clip to the Trash if you're in the Clip Viewer. Or, you can choose Cut or Clear from the Edit menu.

12

EFFECTS

By now, you're probably sold on the notion of working with digital footage, but just in case there are any lingering doubts, consider iMovie's effects capabilities. Because you're manipulating pixels instead of strips of film, you can apply several types of changes to your footage, ranging from color correction to special effects.

When I first heard that iMovie offered effects, I admit I feared the worst. What better way to destroy footage you worked so hard to shoot than to apply a bunch of filters to mangle those pixels? I'm happy to report that my fears were unfounded. Instead of garish methods of swirling video into a toilet bowl of colors, iMovie gives you genuinely useful and powerful tools to adjust color, sharpen blurry images, and easily turn your multi-hued images into classic-looking black-and-white footage.

To view a gallery of iMovie's seven effects, including the extra five in Apple's iMovie Plug-in Pack, see Appendix C.

Editing Effects

Like transitions and titles (see the previous two chapters), iMovie effects are accessed from their own Effects panel (**Figure 12.1**). Clicking an effect's name displays the effect in the preview window; clicking the Preview button shows a rough version of the effect in the Monitor.

Some effects, such as Black and White, don't contain any additional controls; others, such as Adjust Colors, involve several sliders that determine the effect's end result. All of them, however, let you apply or remove the effect gradually.

To control how an effect begins and ends:

1. Select an effect's name in the list.

2. Move the Effect In and Effect Out sliders to control the time it takes for the effect to start and end (**Figure 12.2**). You can, of course, leave them set at zero to apply the effect throughout the entire clip, but changing these values lets you ease into and out of the effect. (For example, suppose you want someone's flashback to appear in black and white, then blend back into color as the flashback merges into the present day.) The times are shown at the bottom of the preview window as you make adjustments.

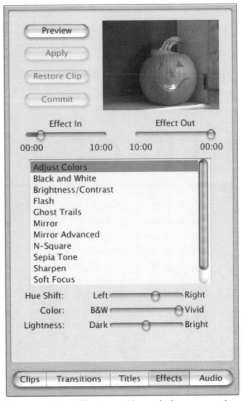

Figure 12.1 The Effects panel is much the same as the Transitions and Titles panels.

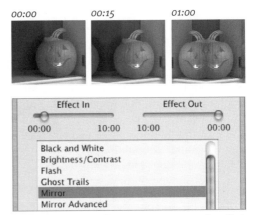

Figure 12.2 Setting Effect In to 01:00 causes the effect to gradually apply, instead of beginning at the start of the clip.

Figure 12.3 Effect-specific controls appear below the list of effects. Changing them updates the preview window dynamically.

To adjust an effect's settings:

1. Select an effect's name in the list. If it features additional controls, they appear below the list (**Figure 12.3**).

2. Move the sliders to adjust the effect's settings. The preview shows your changes immediately, so feel free to experiment.

✔ Tip

■ To reset the sliders to their original positions, click another effect, then switch back to the one you're adjusting. The defaults return when you do, saving you the trouble of trying to approximate the controls' original positions.

This doesn't apply to the Effect In and Effect Out sliders, however. They stay put when you click other effects in the list.

Applying Effects

Editing effects is similar to editing transitions and titles, but the way effects are added to your movie is different. An effect is applied to an entire clip, and alters the clip itself (versus titles, which exist "above" your movie's clips).

To apply an effect:

1. Select the effect you want to apply, and adjust its settings to your liking.

2. Select the clip you want to modify.

3. Click the Apply button in the Effects panel. The clip will begin rendering with the effect applied. In the Clip Viewer, clips with effects are marked with the letters "fx" (**Figure 12.4**).

✔ Tips

- You can reverse steps 1 and 2. Sometimes I select a clip first, sometimes I tinker with effects settings without any clip selected.

- To cancel rendering, press Command-period (.) or choose Undo from the Edit menu.

- If you apply an effect to a still image, the image needs to be converted to a regular clip. Don't worry—iMovie warns you if this is the case, and gives you the option to cancel the action (**Figure 12.5**).

- After you've applied an effect, you can still add transitions or titles to that clip.

Effect indicator

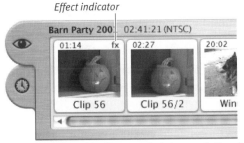

Figure 12.4 Clips with effects applied show up in the Clip Viewer with an "fx" designation.

Figure 12.5 Still images must be converted to regular clips in order to apply effects.

Apply button becomes Update button

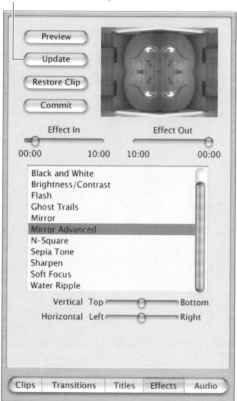

Figure 12.6 Click the Update button after you've modified the effects settings of a clip.

Modifying Existing Effects

After iMovie renders an effect, you can modify its settings without having to start over from scratch.

To update an effect:

1. Select the clip in your movie. The effect's current settings are displayed in the Effects panel.

2. Modify the settings until you're satisfied. Or until a deadline makes it impossible to continue working.

3. When you're finished, click the Update button (which was formerly the Apply button) (**Figure 12.6**).

Removing Effects

On the off chance that you applied several effects in your sleep, waking up in horror to discover that everyone on your spouse's side of the family has been mirrored, there's an easy way to restore those clips. However, you can't simply delete the effect, as you would with a title or transition—deleting the affected clip removes that part of your footage entirely. Instead, use the Restore Clip command.

To remove an effect:

1. Select the clip in your movie.

2. Click the Restore Clip button in the Effects panel (**Figure 12.7**).

✔ Tip

■ Unlike the Restore Clip Media command, which resurrects an entire clip to its state before you applied any edits (covered in Chapter 8), the Restore Clip command in the Effects panel simply removes the effect from that edited portion of the clip.

Restore Clip removes an effect from a clip.

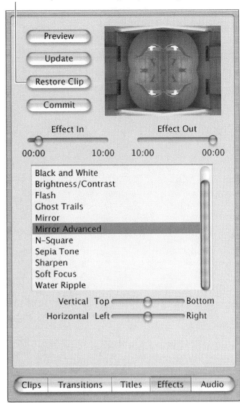

Figure 12.7 You're not deleting a clip's effect so much as you're restoring the clip to its original state.

REMOVING EFFECTS

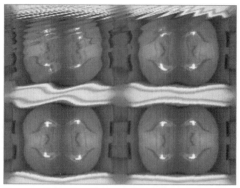

Figure 12.8 On the off chance that you need to apply successive generations of Mirror Advanced, Soft Focus, N-Square, and Water Ripple effects to a clip, you're all set (and a little crazy perhaps).

Click here if you're sure this is the effect for you.

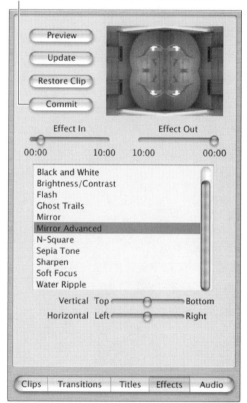

Figure 12.9 Committing an effect renders it to the clip permanently, freeing it up for further effects.

Committing Effects

If you're finished with the clip at this point, you can move on to the next task on your plate. However, there's one more effects command: Commit. When you commit an effect, the only way to change it is to use Undo—you can't specify new settings and click Update, because iMovie considers it to be an original clip, as if you had shot it that way.

Why commit to Commit? You can apply a new effect to the clip once it's committed (such as making a clip black and white, then using Soft Focus to blur it—specifically *not* the example shown in **Figure 12.8**).

To commit an effect:

1. Select the clip in your movie.

2. Click the Commit button (**Figure 12.9**). The clip no longer includes the "fx" designation.

COMMITTING EFFECTS

Part 3
Exporting

MOVING
BACK TO TAPE

Your movie is finished! Now what?

While it's feasible that you could transport your Mac (especially if it's an iBook or PowerBook) to every location where someone might see your movie, that plan runs into a few snags when you want to share your masterpiece with grandparents in Humboldt or your sister in South Africa. Fortunately, getting completed footage out of iMovie is almost as simple as bringing raw footage in.

Exporting to Camera

There are two main advantages to exporting your footage back to your camcorder's DV tape. The camera stores the footage in digital format, so you'll have a copy saved off your computer that retains the same level of quality as what you edited. This is handy in case you need to make a backup of your work so far, or for when you want to hook your camcorder up to a television to show the movie. You can also export your completed movie—which up until now existed as a collection of edited clips—then re-import it into iMovie as one long unbroken clip (depending on length; see Chapter 7) to reclaim some disk space or merge the movie with new footage.

To export to the camera:

1. Switch your camcorder to Play/VCR/VTR mode.

2. Choose Export Movie from iMovie's File menu, or press Command-E. iMovie displays the Export Movie dialog box, with To Camera selected in the Export popup menu (**Figure 13.1**).

3. Enter a number in the field marked Wait [number] seconds for camera to get ready. Your camcorder needs to spin up and get into position before recording, so iMovie will wait for this length of time. If your movies on tape are getting cut off at the beginning, increase this number.

   If you want some black frames before or after your movie, enter numbers in the two remaining fields. This gives you some extra time on the tape and tends to be more professional than just launching into the movie from the beginning.

4. Click the Export button to begin exporting (**Figure 13.2**). When it's finished, iMovie automatically stops the camera.

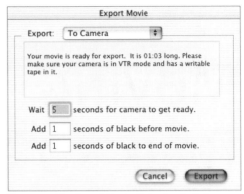

Figure 13.1 The Export Movie dialog box includes controls for setting up the camcorder and adding black frames.

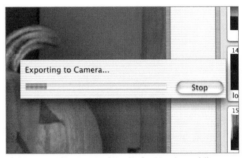

Figure 13.2 The movie plays in the Monitor while you're exporting to the camera.

Figure 13.3 If your movie contains reversed or slow-motion clips, render them before exporting.

Rendering before export

In most cases, exporting to your camcorder is a matter of clicking an OK button, but occasionally iMovie needs to perform a little work beforehand: if your movie contains any clips that have been reversed or slowed down, iMovie prefers to first render those clips to avoid flickering when you play back the video.

To render your movie before exporting:

1. Switch your camcorder to Play/VCR/VTR mode.

2. Choose Export Movie from iMovie's File menu, or press Command-E. The Export Movie dialog box notifies you that some clips need to be rendered (**Figure 13.3**).

3. If iMovie displays a message in the dialog box that your movie needs rendering, click the Render Now button. Depending on the number of clips to render, this operation could take several minutes.

4. When rendering is complete, enter the other export settings and click the Export button.

✔ Tip

■ Exporting your footage to tape serves another important function: providing a backup of your work. Even a modest iMovie project will swamp most backup capacities (such as DAT tape systems) due to the sheer number of gigabytes needed to be backed up. Instead, export your movie to DV tape. In the event that you suffer a hard disk crash (trust me, it's not a fun experience), you won't have your iMovie project, but you'll be able to re-import the edited footage and not lose all of your work.

EXPORTING TO CAMERA

Combining Movie Segments

It's often a good idea to break up a longer movie into smaller segments, working on 10- or 20-minute chunks at a time. But when 10 minutes of footage takes up nearly 11 GB, you simply may not have enough storage space, even with today's bigger hard drives.

To combine movie segments:

1. Export each segment to DV tape using the steps on the previous pages. It's helpful to add a few seconds of black frames to the end of each segment, then rewind the tape a bit so the next segment plays right on the heels of the previous one.

2. Create a new iMovie project by choosing New Project from the File menu. Make sure you have enough hard disk space to accommodate the segments you wish to combine.

3. Switch to Camera Mode and import the segments. Depending on how you've split the segments, you may only have to add a simple transition between them to create a unified whole (**Figure 13.4**).

✔ Tip

- If you're confident that you've finished editing the segments individually, consider importing them as long clips instead of letting iMovie try to split out each scene. In iMovie's preferences, turn off Automatically start new clip at scene break (**Figure 13.5**).

Fade In   Fade Out

Figure 13.4 A pair of Fade In and Fade Out transitions elegantly bridges these two long segments.

Figure 13.5 Turn off the option to Automatically start new clip at scene break to import your segment as one long clip.

Are You Really Ready?

The downside to this approach is that you need to make sure your movie segments are finished (or close enough to being done), because when you re-import them into iMovie, you won't have the clips of unused footage from the individual projects at your disposal.

However, you can always bring in selected media footage using the Import File command under the File menu.

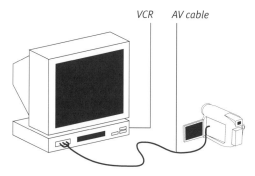

Figure 13.6 Connect your camcorder to a VCR using the AV cable included with the camcorder.

Figure 13.7 iMovie notifies you if you try to export a movie with no tape in the camcorder.

Transferring to Videotape

Until everyone has a DVD player, and until Macs with DVD burners are cheap, the best way to share your movies is still videotape. You can record from your camcorder, or transfer directly from iMovie.

To transfer from your camcorder:

1. Export your movie from iMovie to your camcorder's tape as discussed on the previous pages.

2. Connect your camcorder to a VCR using the AV cables that came with the camcorder (**Figure 13.6**).

3. Switch the camcorder to Play/VCR/VTR mode if it's not already on.

4. Put a blank videotape in the VCR, and rewind the camcorder's tape to the beginning of your movie.

5. Push Record on the VCR.

6. Push Play on the camcorder.

7. When the movie is finished, push Stop on both machines.

To transfer directly from iMovie:

1. Connect your camcorder and VCR as described above.

2. Connect the camcorder to your Mac via FireWire, if it's not already connected.

3. In iMovie's preferences, turn on the Video Play Through to Camera option.

4. Remove the tape from the camcorder, then choose Export from the File menu. A dialog box notifies you that there's no tape (**Figure 13.7**).

5. Press Record on your VCR, and click the Export button in iMovie.

6. When the movie is finished, push Stop on the VCR.

QuickTime
and the Web

On the surface, QuickTime is a great little utility for playing movies on your Mac. I often visit `www.apple.com/trailers/` to see which new movie trailer is ready for download—I click a link, and in a couple of minutes the clip is playing. (It's amazing what you can learn about filmmaking from trailers; they're some of the best sources for how to present ideas and images in a short time span.) Sometimes the movie appears in a window in your Web browser, while other times the QuickTime Player plays the movie.

Now, you have the opportunity to export your movies to the QuickTime format. In so doing, you gain a number of advantages: your file sizes become much smaller (a 1-minute clip can easily shrink from around 200 MB to 2 MB without destroying its quality); your movies can be played on any Macintosh sold within the last four or five years; and you can upload them to the Web, where anyone with a Web browser and the QuickTime software (that includes Windows users, too) can download and view the movie.

You can choose one of iMovie's recommended settings or configure the details yourself to tweak performance. And when it comes time to put the file on the Web, several methods are available, from building a `mac.com` Web page to hand-coding the HTML yourself.

Exporting to QuickTime

Exporting your movie to QuickTime can be as straightforward or as complicated as you want it to be. Understanding that most users won't wade into the complexities of what the QuickTime format can offer, iMovie gives you five pre-configured settings. Following are the basic steps for creating a QuickTime movie from your footage; the intricacies of what QuickTime can do are on the next page.

To export as a QuickTime movie:

1. Choose Export Movie from the File menu.

2. In the Export Movie dialog box, select a format from the Formats popup menu (**Figure 14.1**). These are some common settings for various types of distribution (such as Web versus CD-ROM). See "Choosing a QuickTime format" below for explanations and examples of each.

3. If you want people on older Macs to view your movie, click the box labeled Quick-Time 3.0 Compatible. Note that this can increase the file size of your movie.

4. Click the Export button to begin creating the QuickTime movie.

Choosing a QuickTime format

When you're exporting to QuickTime, remember to keep your audience in mind. You may create a cinematic masterpiece, but if it's several hundred megabytes in size, it likely won't be downloaded over the Web or fit onto a CD-ROM easily. iMovie offers five preset export configurations (**Figures 14.2** and **14.3**); the specifications for each are shown in **Table 14.1**.

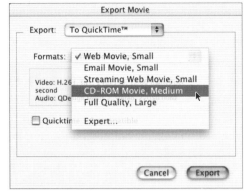

Figure 14.1 iMovie includes five presets for exporting movies in the QuickTime format.

Email Movie, Small

Web Movie, Small
Streaming Web Movie, Small

CD-ROM Movie, Medium

Full Quality, Large

Figure 14.2 This should give you an idea of how the QuickTime export settings compare in iMovie. These images are roughly 25 percent of actual size.

Email Movie, Small

Web Movie, Small

CD-ROM Movie, Medium

Full Quality, Large

Figure 14.3 The different QuickTime export formats vary in visual quality too, based on how much compression is applied with the Image Settings options.

◆ **Web Movie, Small.** At first glance, it looks as if iMovie orders its formats from smallest to largest, but in fact this format is the second-smallest one. Web Movie is a good compromise between file size and video quality.

◆ **Email Movie, Small.** This is the smallest format available from the presets, and represents quite a sacrifice of quality in favor of small file sizes. Don't expect titles to be read easily, but do expect speed: this movie can be half the size of a Web Movie.

◆ **Streaming Web Movie, Small.** A movie that's streamed is played as it downloads, so you don't have to wait for the entire movie to arrive before viewing it. Slightly larger in file size than the Web Movie above, this format includes data that enables the movie to be streamed from a dedicated streaming server (versus downloaded as a file, then played back).

◆ **CD-ROM Movie, Medium.** The CD-ROM Movie format increases the file size quite a bit from the Web Movie, but the quality differences are immediately apparent. Note that the "CD-ROM" designation refers to file size, not a requirement that it can only be used on CD-ROMs.

continues on next page

Table 14.1

iMovie's Stock Compression Settings

iMovie Format	Video Compression	Size (pixels)	Frame Rate	Audio Compression	Stereo/ Mono	Sample Rate	Sample File Size*
Web Movie, Small	H.263	240 x 180	12.00 fps	QDesign Music 2	Stereo	22050.00 Hz	2.0 MB
Email Movie, Small	H.263	160 x 120	10.00 fps	QDesign Music 2	Mono	22050.00 Hz	1.0 MB
Streaming Web Movie, Small	H.263	240 x 180	12.00 fps	QDesign Music 2	Stereo	22050.00 Hz	2.2 MB
CD-ROM Movie, Medium	H.263	320 x 240	15.00 fps	IMA 4:1	Stereo	44100.00 Hz	5.8 MB
Full Quality, Large	DV - NTSC	720 x 480	29.97 fps	No compression	Stereo	48000.00 Hz	216.8 MB

* File size is based on exporting the sample one-minute movie found on the previous page.

EXPORTING TO QUICKTIME

◆ **Full Quality, Large.** This format should
be titled "Full Quality, HUGE" due to its
massive file size. What makes it so big?
It's the same format as what your camera
produces, so you're looking at essentially
uncompressed footage. It's big and beautiful, but you take a serious hard disk hit
(about 200 MB per minute of video).

✔ Tips

■ Full Quality is the same format as the DV
files found in your project's Media folder.
If you want to export your movie to the
hard disk instead of to tape (see Chapter
13), use Full Quality to create a new DV
file. This is also what you'd do to create
footage for import into more advanced
programs such as Apple's Final Cut Pro.
Make sure you have plenty of disk space,
though!

■ Why is the video size for Full Quality set
to 720 x 480, instead of the Monitor's size
of 640 x 480? You know that each frame is
composed of pixels, but what's not obvious is that the pixels in digital video are
rectangular (taller than they are wide, as
shown in **Figure 14.4**).

Similarly, the frame rate of 29.97 fps isn't
rounded up to 30 fps. Way back when the
first color televisions were introduced,
the frame rate needed to be adjusted
slightly to avoid audio distortion—and
the setting stuck.

Full Quality, Large (720 x 480 pixels)

Full Quality, Large (640 x 480 pixels)

Figure 14.4 The Full Quality format exports
video measuring 720 x 480 pixels, compared to
the 640 x 480 pixel size you're accustomed to. If
you were to import it into another video-editing
application, it would appear as 640 x 480 (just
like in iMovie).

Video Compression Terms You Should Know

Codec: Short for compression/decompression; another name for a compressor.

Compression: The method used to reduce the size of the movie file while still retaining image quality. Video and audio compression are a tricky business: you have to weigh the benefits of smaller file sizes (and therefore potentially faster downloads) against the desire to have the best-looking movies possible. There are many methods of compression available, each with its own strengths. **Table 14.2** on the next page provides an overview of the compressors available when exporting from iMovie. There are more available if you export files from QuickTime Player Pro, and still more offered by professional editing packages such as Cleaner 5 (www.discreet.com).

Data Rate: The amount of data sent from one point to another during a given time, such as the number of kilobytes delivered during a Web download.

Frame Rate: The number of frames displayed during 1 second. As more frames are included, the movie will play smoother—but adding frames increases the size of the file. Uncompressed DV video runs at 30 frames per second (fps); a typical QuickTime movie can contain 15 or 12 frames per second.

Key Frame: A complete movie frame that acts as the image base for successive frames. Unlike film, which displays 24 full frames per second on a reel of celluloid, QuickTime compares most of the frames in a movie with its key frames and notes the differences. Although this sounds like more work than just displaying each frame in its entirety, it actually means the movie player is drawing less data.

For example, consider a clip where the camera is stationary, filming a person talking. Every pixel of the first frame, the key frame, is drawn; in the next frame, the only change is that the person's lips have moved. Instead of redrawing the background and everything else, QuickTime holds onto the first frame and only changes the pixels around the person's mouth. So, the second frame (and third, fourth, and so on) contain only a few pixels' worth of information, dramatically reducing the total amount of data required and creating a smaller file. Of course, the entire movie likely won't be composed of just the person talking, so QuickTime creates several key frames along the way, allowing the player to regroup and start over. The more key frames that appear in your movie, the larger the file size will be.

Sample Rate: The quality of audio, measured in hertz (Hz). The higher the number, the more audio data is present, and therefore the better the quality of sound.

Exporting to QuickTime Using Expert Settings

iMovie's stock QuickTime format settings are good for most situations, but you can also use other compression formats and options by way of the Expert option under the Formats popup menu (**Table 14.2**).

Table 14.2

Video Compressors Included with QuickTime 5*	
COMPRESSOR NAME	**COMMENTS**
Animation	Works best on computer-generated animations with broad areas of flat color. Doesn't work well for scenes with lots of color changes.
BMP	Used for still images to be exported in BMP format. Does minimal compression. Inappropriate for video-based movie playback.
Cinepak	Commonly used for video movies that require CD-ROM playback. Compresses very slowly.
Component Video	High-quality compressor. Good for capture on Macs with built-in video capture capabilities and for use as an intermediate storage format. Low compression ratios (larger files).
DV-NTSC, DV-PAL	Used with Digital Video cameras.
Graphics	Good for 8-bit graphics files. Usually better than the Animation compressor in 8 bits. Slower to decompress than Animation.
H.261	Originally designed for videoconferencing. Extremely high compression ratios.
H.263	Originally designed for videoconferencing. Very high compression ratios. Sometimes good for Web video.
Intel Indeo Video 4.4	High image quality. Requires a Pentium processor for compression and decompression. Mac OS version is not built into QuickTime but can be downloaded from www.apple.com/quicktime/technologies/indeo/.
Motion JPEG A, Motion JPEG B	Used to decompress files made with certain Motion-JPEG cards when the card isn't available or to compress in a format that can be played by certain hardware Motion-JPEG cards.
None	Good for capture only. Does almost no compression.
Photo JPEG	Ideal for high-quality compressed still images. Also useful as an intermediate storage format for movies and QuickTime VR panoramas. Decompresses too slowly for video-based playback.
Planar RGB	For images with an alpha channel.
PNG	Typically used for still-image compression. Can get high compression ratios.
Sorenson Video	Very high compression ratios and high quality. Excellent for Web and CD-ROM.
Sorenson Video 3	Very high compression ratios and very high quality (better than Sorenson Video). Currently the best choice for Web and CD-ROM.
Targa	Typically used for still-image compression. Does minimal compression.
TIFF	Typically used for still-image compression. Does minimal compression.
Video	Very fast video compression and decompression. Decent compression ratios. Good for real-time capture of video, particularly when hard disk space is at a premium. Good for testing clips. OK for hard disk playback. Image quality is poor when compressing enough for CD-ROM playback.

Note: The Minimum Install of QuickTime (which many users will choose) doesn't install all these compressors. If the computer being used to play a movie that requires one of these compressors has an Internet connection, QuickTime downloads the necessary compressor when it is needed for decompression.

* This table originally appeared in *QuickTime 5 for Macintosh and Windows: Visual QuickStart Guide*, by Judith Stern and Robert Lettieri, and is used here with their permission. See www.judyandrobert.com/quicktime/ for more information.

Figure 14.5 The Expert QuickTime Settings provide many more options for controlling the compression.

Figure 14.6 Clicking the 4:3 box forces the Width and Height values to make sure your video isn't distorted vertically or horizontally after you export it.

Figure 14.7 The Compression Settings dialog box lets you tweak the QuickTime output even more.

To change Image Settings:

1. Choose Export Movie from the File menu, or press Command-E.

2. In the Export Movie dialog box, choose Expert from the Formats popup menu. The Expert QuickTime Settings dialog box appears (**Figure 14.5**).

3. In the Image Settings portion of the window, enter width and height values to specify a new size. Clicking the 4:3 box adjusts the numbers so that the image stays in proportion (**Figure 14.6**).

4. Click the Settings button to display the Compression Settings dialog box, where you can fine-tune the type and amount of compression applied (**Figure 14.7**).

5. In the Compressor area, choose a compression method from the first popup menu. The second popup menu specifies how many colors to use when exporting the file (fewer colors equal more compression, but lower image quality).

6. Move the Quality slider to the lowest level you can that maintains good image quality; the thumbnail in the upper-right corner of the dialog box shows you how much compression is being applied.

7. In the Motion area, select the number of frames per second from the popup menu beside the field, or just enter a value.

8. Enter a number in the Key frame every [number] frames field to set how often a key frame is generated. If you don't want iMovie to generate key frames (i.e., every frame is a full frame), deselect this option.

continues on next page

9. To target a specific data rate, enter a value in the field labeled Limit data rate to [number] KBytes/sec.

10. Click OK to return to the Expert QuickTime Settings dialog box.

✔ Tips

■ To get a sense for how the compressors compare, create a short movie (30 seconds or so) that's representative of your footage and export it using the various formats, and compare the results.

■ The Sorenson Video codecs are highly regarded for having high video quality with good compression. For some suggested Sorenson settings, select iMovie Help from the Help menu and search for "Sorenson Codec".

QuickTime versus QuickTime Pro

Every Mac comes with QuickTime, including the free QuickTime Player, which allows you to play back QuickTime movies and a host of other file formats (ranging from MPEG-formatted movies to MP3 audio files). If you're serious about optimizing your QuickTime movies for the Web, however, consider paying the $30 for a QuickTime Pro license, which turns QuickTime Player into a sophisticated movie editor. Not only does it give you an easy way to resize or recompress QuickTime movies, it also lets you save your movies into other formats, such as AVI, which Windows users can view if they don't have QuickTime installed.

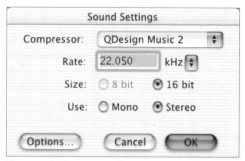

Figure 14.8 Choose an audio compressor to fine-tune how your movie's audio sounds after exporting.

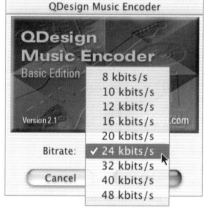

Figure 14.9 Some compressors include other settings to help reduce your movie's file without sacrificing too much quality.

To change audio settings:

1. Choose Export Movie from the File menu, or press Command-E.

2. In the Export Movie dialog box, choose Expert from the Formats popup menu. The Expert QuickTime Settings dialog box appears.

3. In the Audio Settings portion of the window, click the Settings button to display the Sound Settings dialog box (**Figure 14.8**).

4. Choose a format from the Compressor popup menu. Some of the compressors include further settings, which are accessed by clicking the Options button. These usually determine how the data is encoded or specify a data rate (or bit rate) (**Figure 14.9**).

5. In the Rate field, type in a kHz value or select one from the popup menu to the right. Lower kHz settings will degrade the sound quality.

6. Click either the 8 bit or 16 bit button to determine how much audio data is included in the file. The higher number provides for better sound quality, but at the expense of a larger file size.

7. Decide whether the audio will play back in stereo or mono by checking a button next to the Use option. Stereo sounds better, but Mono offers a smaller file size.

8. Click OK to return to the Expert Quick-Time Settings dialog box.

EXPORTING USING EXPERT SETTINGS

To prepare a movie for Internet streaming:

1. Choose Export Movie from the File menu, or press Command-E.

2. In the Export Movie dialog box, choose Expert from the Formats popup menu. The Expert QuickTime Settings dialog box appears.

3. Click the Prepare for Internet box in the lower-right corner (**Figure 14.10**).

4. From the popup menu, select QuickTime Streaming Server if you'll be using that type of server to host your movie; if not, choose Standard Web Server.

✔ Tip

■ Trust me when I say that everything described so far in this chapter is really just the tip of a very large iceberg. If you're willing to shell out the bucks, software such as Cleaner 5 can encode and compress your movies into nearly any possible movie format, with more control than can be found in iMovie's or QuickTime Player's export features. Look at the videos Apple makes available on its Web site, including theatrical movie trailers and product commercials, to see how high-end editing and video compression tools can make a huge difference in the quality of a movie while creating a small file (www.apple.com/quicktime/).

Figure 14.10 To enable Web streaming, click the Prepare for Internet box and choose a server type.

Figure 14.11 You spent all that time editing—put your movies on the Web where others can see (for example, homepage.mac.com/jeffc/ shown here).

Getting Your Movie on the Web

You may be creating movies that will live only on your hard disk, for your eyes only, never to be seen by anyone. More likely, though, your movies are meant to be viewed. As we've covered already, you can export the movie to a videotape and mail it to your relatives—if you don't mind purchasing the tape, filling it with movies (or just using a few minutes of it for one movie), then paying to mail it across the country or around the world. Where's the instant gratification in that? Instead (or in addition), post your movie to the Web (**Figure 14.11**), where anyone can download and view your creation within minutes of its completion (and which is also available 24 hours a day, perfect for your uncle who likes to work online at 2 a.m.).

When putting movies online, keep your audience in mind: do they have fast broadband connections like DSL or cable, or are they connecting with dialup modems? That will affect which format you export the movie to. The settings for Web Movie, Small provide a decent trade-off between quality and compression, but it may be easier for some folks to handle the Email Movie, Small format instead. (Or, if you have the storage space on your server, consider making multiple versions so your audience can decide which size is best for them.)

If you use a Web design program such as Adobe GoLive or Macromedia Dreamweaver, follow the instructions for adding Quick-Time movies to your pages. For our purposes here, I'm going to assume that you don't own a Web design application and instead want to either post a movie on the Web for free using Apple's simple Web-based iTools, or hand-code the HTML (HyperText Markup Language) necessary to make the movie appear on a Web page.

Apple's iTools

These days, the easiest method for putting your movies on the Web is to use Apple's iTools (itools.mac.com). When you sign up for a free membership, you gain access to an iDisk, which is essentially a networked 20 MB hard drive that lives at Apple. You also get to use the online Homepage tools to create a site, and a mac.com email thrown into the mix, too. Once you've created an account, you simply copy your movie to a folder in your iDisk, then use it to build a Web page.

To mount your iDisk (Mac OS 9, Chooser method):

1. Go to the Apple menu and select Chooser.

2. Click the AppleShare icon in the left pane (**Figure 14.12**).

3. Click the Server IP Address button.

4. Type idisk.mac.com and click Connect.

To mount your iDisk (Mac OS 9, Web method):

1. Launch a Web browser and enter itools.mac.com in the Address field. This connects you to Apple's iTools page (**Figure 14.13**).

2. Click the iDisk icon.

3. Log in to iTools with the user name and password you used when you registered.

4. Click the Open Your iDisk link. The iDisk appears on your Desktop (**Figure 14.14**).

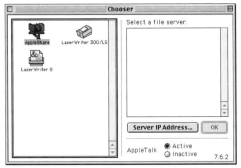

Figure 14.12 The AppleShare access in the Chooser includes the capability to enter an Internet address directly using the Server IP Address button.

iDisk icon

Figure 14.13 Click the iDisk button on the iTools Web page to access your personal disk.

Figure 14.14 When you click the Open Your iDisk button on the iDisk Web page, your disk appears on the Desktop like any other hard disk (right).

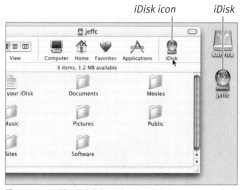

iDisk icon   iDisk

Figure 14.15 The iDisk icon in Mac OS X permanently resides in the Toolbar of your windows.

Figure 14.16 You can also take a textual approach by typing the iDisk address in the Connect to Server dialog box.

Figure 14.17 To make a movie file available to iTools, copy it from its location on your hard disk (top) to the Movies folder of your iDisk (bottom).

To mount your iDisk (Mac OS X):

◆ Click the iDisk link in the Toolbar (**Figure 14.15**). Your iDisk appears on the Desktop.

or

1. In the Finder, choose Connect to Server from the Go menu (or press Command-K).

2. Type `afp://idisk.mac.com` in the Address field, and click the Connect button (**Figure 14.16**).

3. Enter your user name and password. The iDisk appears on the Desktop.

To copy a movie to your iDisk:

1. Double-click your iDisk to open it. Inside, you'll see a folder titled Movies.

2. Drag and drop your QuickTime movie file on the Movies folder (**Figure 14.17**). After the file copies to your iDisk, it will be available to the Homepage module of iTools.

APPLE'S ITOOLS

To build a Web page using iTools:

1. Launch a Web browser and enter itools.mac.com in the Address field to connect to Apple's iTools page (if you're not already connected).

2. Click the Homepage icon.

3. Log in to iTools with the user name and password you used when you registered.

4. In the area marked Create a page, click the iMovies tab (**Figure 14.18**).

5. Click a theme that will surround the movie, such as a drive-in theater or retro-TV. A preview of the page appears.

6. Click the Edit button at the top of the page, which loads the same page but with editable text fields.

7. Type the page title, movie title, and page description text in the fields provided.

8. Click the Choose button below the movie placeholder to select your movie. You will be redirected to a new page listing the movie files located in your iDisk's Movies folder (**Figure 14.19**).

9. Click the name of the movie file you want to use, then click the Choose button. You will be taken back to the editing page.

10. Click the Preview button to see what it will look like, or click the Publish button to create the new page. iTools will then display the URL of the page that you can send to other people.

✔ Tips

■ iTools automatically prepares your movie for Web streaming after you copy it to your iDisk.

■ To see a large collection of movies created by iMovie users, check out Apple's gallery at www.apple.com/imovie/gallery/.

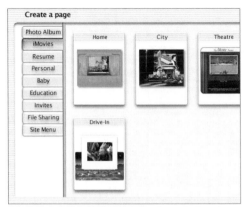

Figure 14.18 iTools includes several pre-designed templates for Web pages, such as for iMovies.

Figure 14.19 Click the Preview button to play the movie highlighted in the list at left.

APPLE'S ITOOLS

HTML text that creates link

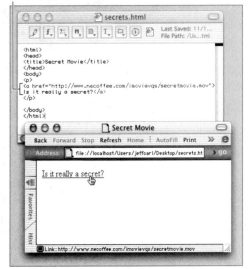

Figure 14.20 Add a simple Web link that points to your QuickTime movie file. The HTML text in the top window creates the Web page in the bottom window.

Writing HTML

This, of course, isn't a book about HTML, so I'm going to assume that you know the basics about coding Web pages, and that you have an application (such as Bare Bones Software's BBEdit, or even SimpleText or TextEdit) that you use to build pages. If that's not the case, check out Elizabeth Castro's book *HTML 4 for the World Wide Web: Visual QuickStart Guide*, which remains the best HTML guide I've read (I said so even before I got involved with Peachpit Press).

That said, there are still some important things to know about adding a movie to a Web page using HTML. There are two ways of going about it: you can copy the file to your Web directory (provided by your Internet service provider) then link directly to it; or you can embed the movie on a Web page so that it's part of the page's layout.

To link to a QuickTime movie file:

1. In your HTML editing application, enter the following code where you want your movie link to appear. The user will see only the linked text; clicking it will down-load the movie.

    ```
    <a href="http://www.youraddress.com/
    sample.mov">Click here</a>
    ```

2. Insert the real names of your Web address and movie filename in place of *youraddress.com* and *sample.mov* (**Figure 14.20**). For example, a movie on my Web site would look like this (go ahead and put the URL below into your Web browser to view the movie).

    ```
    <a href="http://www.necoffee.com/
    imovievqs/secretmovie.mov">Is it
    really a secret?</a>
    ```

To embed the movie on a page:

◆ In your HTML editing application, enter
the following code where you want the
movie to appear. Be sure to change the
two instances of `sample.mov` to your
actual file name, plus the two instances
where the width and height are defined.

```
<OBJECT CLASSID="clsid:02BF25D5-8C17-
4B23-BC80-D3488ABDDC6B" WIDTH="160"
HEIGHT="144"
CODEBASE="http://www.apple.com/
qtactivex/qtplugin.cab">
<PARAM name="SRC" VALUE="sample.mov">
<PARAM name="AUTOPLAY" VALUE="true">
<PARAM name="CONTROLLER"
VALUE="false">
<EMBED SRC="sample.mov" WIDTH="160"
HEIGHT="144" AUTOPLAY="true"
CONTROLLER="false" PLUGINSPAGE=
"http://www.apple.com/quicktime/
download/">
</EMBED>
</OBJECT>
```

Note that the unintelligible gobbledygook
following "CLASSID=" must be entered
exactly as shown; it's required for viewing
the page properly in Microsoft Internet
Explorer 5.5 and later under Windows
(see the tip on the next page).

Deciphering HTML Attributes

So what is all that junk I threw in there?
Here's a breakdown of the tag attributes:

OBJECT CLASSID: To work properly
under Windows, a QuickTime movie must
be defined as an object. The CLASSID
value identifies the content as a Quick-
Time movie.

WIDTH and **HEIGHT:** These values tell
the browser the width and height of your
movie in pixels.

CODEBASE: This URL gives Internet
Explorer for Windows some necessary
information about the QuickTime format.

PARAM: This is a parameter of the
object, which consists of a name and a
value. SRC is the URL that points to your
movie file; AUTOPLAY tells the browser
whether to automatically play the movie
when it loads (in this case "true" means
yes); CONTROLLER tells the browser
whether to display the QuickTime controller beneath the movie (in this case
"false" means no).

EMBED: This is the tag that actually
puts your QuickTime movie on the page.
It includes the same attributes as PARAM,
though in a slightly more compact fashion. A Web page that contains only this
tag will display the movie correctly in all
Web browsers except Internet Explorer
5.5 and later for Windows.

PLUGINSPAGE: This tells the browser
where to go in the event that the Quick-
Time plug-in is not installed.

</EMBED> and **</OBJECT>:** These are
closing tags, indicating the end of the
commands.

✔ Tip

- If you know how to embed an object already, you may be wondering why this example contains so much other information. In late 2001, Microsoft stopped supporting the plug-in architecture used by Web browsers since long before Microsoft even got into the browser business (when a QuickTime movie appears on a page, a QuickTime plug-in—not the browser by itself—is doing the work of playing it back correctly). Instead, Microsoft switched to its own ActiveX architecture—but only under Internet Explorer 5.5 and later for Windows. So although movies added using the regular method of embedding objects still work on your Mac, anyone with a recent version of Windows likely won't be able to see it. Hence, the added code. Find more information at `developer.apple.com/quicktime/compatibility.html`.

Creating a Poster Movie

Accessing a QuickTime movie on the Web introduces one big problem: whether you link to it directly or embed it onto a page, the entire movie begins downloading. Depending on the size of the movie, this could slow your browser or other Internet applications while the movie is being fetched.

As an alternative, create a poster movie, which displays a one-frame movie that your visitors can click to initiate the download. (Sometimes this can be frustrating: I've clicked on links expecting the movie to load in the background while I'm working on something else, only to realize that I needed to then click the poster movie to get the download started. Still, at least this route gives the visitor the option to start the movie at her convenience.) The poster movie has the added benefit of preloading the Quick-Time plug-in before the movie starts.

Creating a poster movie involves two steps: creating the one-frame movie using Quick-Time Player (the Pro version), then adjusting the EMBED tag in the HTML to properly handle it.

To create the poster movie:

1. Open your movie in QuickTime Player.

2. Use the movie control buttons or the location indicator to find a frame you'd like to use as the poster movie's image (**Figure 14.21**).

3. Choose Copy from the Edit menu, or press Command-C. This copies the selected frame.

4. Create a new movie by choosing New (Command-N) from the File menu.

Figure 14.21 Use the playhead in QuickTime Player to locate the frame you'd like to use for the poster movie.

Figure 14.22 To make the poster movie work, your one frame needs to be saved as a QuickTime movie, not an individual image format like TIFF or JPEG.

Figure 14.23 The end result is a single image that shows up in place of the movie, but one you can click to immediately begin playing the movie.

5. Choose Paste (Command-V) from the Edit menu. Your copied frame appears as its own one-frame movie (**Figure 14.22**).

6. Save the movie with a distinctive name, such as "punkins_cdrom_poster.mov" (to use my example).

To embed the poster movie:

1. In your HTML editor, type the code you used to embed the movie (shown three pages back).

2. In the EMBED tag, add the HREF and TARGET attributes (underlined):

```
<EMBED SRC="sample.mov" WIDTH="160"
HEIGHT="144" AUTOPLAY="true"
CONTROLLER="false"
HREF="sample_poster.mov"
TARGET="myself" PLUGINSPAGE=
"http://www.apple.com/quicktime/
download/">
```

The HREF tag tells the browser to first load the poster movie, while the TARGET tag instructs it to play the real movie in the same space as the poster movie when clicked.

3. Save and upload your files. When you view them in a Web browser, the poster image shows up first (**Figure 14.23**).

✔ Tips

■ If you're seeing only half of the movie controller, add 15 to the height values in the OBJECT and EMBED tags.

■ Be sure the controller attributes are set to "false," or else you'll see a controller in the poster movie, which can be confusing. Viewers might click the controller to play the movie, which works—but only plays the one frame.

■ It's a good idea to include instructions near the poster movie that say something like, "Click to play movie."

EXPORTING TO DVD

My father has amassed a fairly large video-tape collection over the past several years. So you can imagine that he's done a fair bit of eye-rolling as DVD discs have quickly gained in popularity, because now he has to decide whether he wants to begin building a DVD collection, too.

In the case of DVDs, it's going to be a hard sell to hold on to old VHS tapes. The single advantage videotape holds is that VHS players are still much more common than DVD players. But that won't be the case for long.

DVD has several key advantages over VHS. The discs are smaller than videotapes, image and sound quality are much better, and discs don't degrade over time (at least, not remotely as fast as tape, a fact you're no doubt aware of if you have an aging wedding or graduation video sitting on a shelf). And DVDs are interactive: jump to your favorite scene in a movie; play a director's commentary while watching a movie; or, in the case of making and playing iMovie videos, store several movies on one disc that can be accessed without fast-forwarding (and rewinding, then fast-forwarding again as you try to find the beginning on a tape).

This chapter explains how you can easily export your footage from iMovie and bring it into the equally easy-to-use iDVD software.

Exporting for iDVD

Apple expects that at some point everyone will have a Mac equipped with a DVD-R drive (DVD-Recordable, which Apple calls a SuperDrive). If you do own one of these machines, you can use iDVD.

However, at this writing iDVD 2 will *only* run on a SuperDrive-equipped Mac running Mac OS X 10.1 or later. So if you have any other Mac, you may have to export your movie for iDVD, then find a friend or service bureau with the correct hardware.

To export for iDVD:

1. Choose Export Movie from the File menu.

2. In the Export Movie dialog box, choose For iDVD from the Export popup menu. If you have any clips that are reversed or in slow motion, you can choose to render them by clicking the Render Now button (**Figure 15.1**).

3. Click the Export button to export the movie.

4. Name the movie file and choose a location, then click the Save button. iMovie saves it as a DV-formatted QuickTime movie.

✔ Tip

■ Do those export specs look familiar? The iDVD option is exactly the same as the Full Quality, Large option when exporting as a QuickTime file (see Chapter 14). The only difference here is that you don't have the option to specify custom video and audio settings. You could just as easily export your movie as a Full Quality, Large QuickTime movie, but taking the iDVD route is more straightforward.

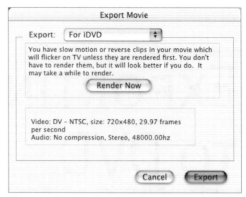

Figure 15.1 Just as when you export your movie to the camera or to QuickTime format, the For iDVD option warns you if some clips need to be rendered.

Figure 15.2 Like iMovie's opening screen, iDVD includes buttons for creating and opening projects.

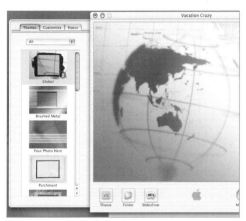

Figure 15.3 Select a theme from the Themes Panel, which pops out from the left side of the main window.

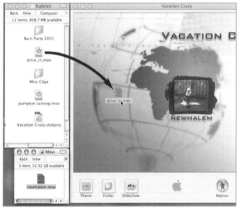

Figure 15.4 Simply drag QuickTime movies from the Finder onto the iDVD main window to add them.

Figure 15.5 When you click a movie, you can set its thumbnail image by dragging the playhead to the frame you want to use.

Creating a DVD in iDVD

If you think iMovie is easy to master, wait until you spend five minutes with iDVD.

To build a project in iDVD:

1. Launch iDVD.

2. On the title screen, click the New Project button to create and name your project (**Figure 15.2**). Or, choose New Project from the File menu.

3. Select a theme by clicking the Theme button and choosing one from the Themes Panel that pops out from the left side of the main window (**Figure 15.3**).

4. Click the title in the main screen and retype a new one if you want.

5. Position the iDVD window so that you can see the movie files you wish to add.

6. Drag and drop a movie file to the iDVD window (**Figure 15.4**).

7. Click the name of your movie and type a new name if you want (which is better than having movies named "movie.mov").

8. (This is my favorite feature.) With your movie selected, drag the playhead that appears above it to select a frame to be used as the movie's thumbnail (**Figure 15.5**). If you want the movie to play in the preview, click the Movie button. You're not stuck with the first frame of your movie (which is often just an empty frame)—and best of all, you don't have to export a frame from iMovie, modify it in an image editing application, and bring it back in to use as a still image.

Repeat the steps above for each movie you want to add to your project. iDVD keeps track of how much time your project is occupying in the Status tab of the Theme panel (**Figure 15.6**, on the next page).

CREATING A DVD IN iDVD

✔ Tips

- Click the Preview button to see how the DVD will appear in a DVD player.

- Although you'll get better image quality by importing DV-formatted QuickTime movies into iDVD, you can drag any QuickTime movie into your project. Just remember that movies with more compression won't appear as sharp—but at the same time, if you're willing to sacrifice a little quality, you can store more movies on a single DVD disc.

- iDVD can also create slide shows of photos and still images (like artwork), using the same drag-and-drop approach.

- This chapter focuses on using iDVD to put together a project of your movies, but iDVD isn't required if you want to simply store your movies on a DVD disc. Mac OS 9.2 and Mac OS X 10.1 both feature the capability to drag QuickTime movies (and any other type of file) to a DVD disc for high capacity storage. When you insert the disc into your Mac, you can play the movies in the QuickTime Player. If you take this route, however, you can't view the movies in a consumer DVD player.

To burn the DVD disc:

1. When your project is ready to go, be sure to save it, then insert a blank DVD disc in your Mac's SuperDrive.

2. Choose Burn DVD from the File menu, or click the Burn button (**Figure 15.7**). The burning process takes approximately twice as long as the combined length of your movies.

Figure 15.6 Click the Status tab of the Themes Panel to see how much space you have left before filling up a DVD disc.

Figure 15.7 When you're ready to burn the DVD, click the Burn button and insert a blank disk.

DVD Studio Pro

For much more control over the creation of DVDs, consider moving up to Apple's DVD Studio Pro ($999, www.apple.com/dvdstudiopro/). iDVD is set up to make the process of creating a DVD as easy as possible, with built-in templates and themes. DVD Studio Pro lets you assemble all the rest of the pieces.

Figure 15.8 If DVD Player doesn't start up when you insert a DVD disc, locate and launch the program. Under Mac OS 9, iDVD is located in the folder titled Applications (Mac OS 9). iDVD 2 is available only for Mac OS X, and is located within the Applications folder.

Figure 15.9 Use the floating remote control to begin playing your DVD. You can then navigate the interface with your mouse to click on specific movies.

Playing the DVD

With your DVD created, your work is done and it's time to enjoy the project.

To play the DVD disc in a consumer DVD player:

Insert the disc into your DVD player and push the Play button. Use the remote control to select which movies to play.

To play the DVD disc on your Mac:

1. Insert the DVD disc in your DVD-ROM drive equipped Mac.

2. Depending on how your computer is configured, the DVD Player software may load automatically when the disc is inserted. If it doesn't, locate and launch DVD Player (**Figure 15.8**).

3. Click the Play button on the DVD Player's floating Controller, or choose Play from the Controls menu (**Figure 15.9**).

✔ Tip

- You can play the DVD on PCs running Windows, too. The steps for launching the player software and viewing a disc should be similar.

TRANSITIONS
GALLERY

The best type of transition is one that the viewer doesn't notice. That's why Fade In, Fade Out, and Cross Dissolve are used so prominently in film—they're subtle enough to not scream, "Look at me!" while not as abrupt as a jump cut between scenes.

This appendix contains the transitions available in iMovie 2 and in the iMovie Plug-in Pack. You can download the latter for free at Apple's Web site (www.apple.com/imovie/). Other transitions are available for purchase from Gee Three (www.geethree.com). Since this is a book, not a video, I've broken each transition into four steps to give you an idea of what happens. However, the best way to preview a transition is to click its name in iMovie's Transitions panel.

See Chapter 10 for information on how to apply transitions.

Circle Closing

Circle Opening

Cross Dissolve

Fade In

Fade Out

Overlap

Push

Radial

Scale Down

Warp In

Warp Out

Wash In

Wash Out

TITLES GALLERY

You've heard the expression that a picture is worth a thousand words, but that makes it sound like you can use either pictures *or* words. How about both?

iMovie's titles aren't just words that float at the bottom of your screen. They're animated, they have character, and they're configurable. The titles shown in this appendix include the ones built in to iMovie, plus the ones available in Apple's free iMovie Plug-in Pack (www.apple.com/imovie/). Other titles are available for purchase from Gee Three (www.geethree.com).

I've tried to recreate the title animations using two views, though you can't get the full effect until you click a title's name in iMovie's Titles panel. Yet there were a few, such as Music Video, Subtitle, and Stripe Subtitle, whose appearance is summed up in one view.

For more information about configuring and applying titles, see Chapter 11.

Bounce In To Center

Centered Multiple

Centered Title

Drifting

Flying Letters

Flying Words

 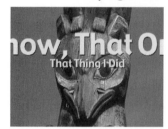

Music Video

Rolling Centered Credits

Rolling Credits

Scroll with Pause

Scrolling Block

 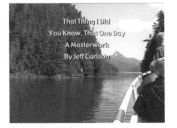

Stripe Subtitle

Subtitle

Subtitle Multiple

Typewriter

Zoom

Zoom Multiple

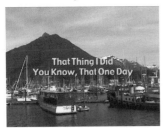 

EFFECTS GALLERY

Using iMovie's effects, you probably won't be mistaken for Industrial Light and Magic, but you will be able to spice up your footage without having to lift a finger.

The effects in this appendix represent the ones built in to iMovie, and also include the effects in the free iMovie Plug-in Pack (www.apple.com/imovie/). Other effects are available for purchase from Gee Three (www.geethree.com).

As you might expect in this grayscale book, it's hard to reproduce the essence of an effect on paper, especially for one such as Black and White. So, I kindly ask that you either use your imagination on the following pages, or go to iMovie's Effects panel and click an effect to view its preview.

For information on how to edit and apply effects, see Chapter 12.

Adjust Colors

Black and White

Brightness/Contrast

Flash

Ghost Trails

Mirror

Mirror Advanced

 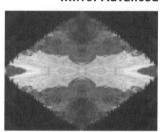

N-Square

Sepia Tone

Sharpen

Soft Focus

Water Ripple

EFFECTS GALLERY

RESOURCES

Essential Information

Apple iMovie

http://www.apple.com/imovie/

iMovie 2 for Macintosh: Visual QuickStart Guide companion Web site

http://www.peachpit.com/vqs/imovie/

Canon Digital Camcorders

http://www.canondv.com/

Sony Digital Camcorders

http://www.sonystyle.com/digitalimaging/
H_Camcorders.shtml

JVC Digital Camcorders

http://www.jvc.com/

Recommended Books

The Computer Videomaker Handbook, by the editors of *Computer Videomaker Magazine* (Focal Press, 2001)

http://www.videomaker.com/

Firewire Filmmaking, Scott Smith (Peachpit Press, 2002)

http://www.peachpit.com/

Online Tutorials and Reference

Cyber Film School

http://www.cyberfilmschool.com/

DVcreators.net

http://www.dvcreators.net/

Post Forum

http://www.postforum.com/

Audio Editing Applications

Coaster

http://www.visualclick.de/products/
coaster/index.html

SoundApp

http://www.spies.com/~franke/SoundApp/

SndSampler

http://www.sndsampler.com/

Royalty Free Audio Clips

Freeplay Music

http://www.freeplaymusic.com/

Killer Sound, Inc.

http://www.killersound.com/

Sound Dogs

http://www.sounddogs.com/

iMovie Plug-ins

GeeThree

http://www.geethree.com/

INDEX

INDEX

INDEX

INDEX

W

Z

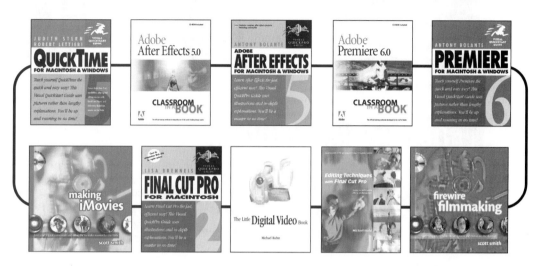

OS X

Watch for these titles: